IT HAPPENED IN
MICKLEOVER

IT HAPPENED IN MICKLEOVER

NORTH BRIDGE PUBLISHING

First published in Great Britain in 2014 by

North Bridge Publishing
20 Chain Lane
Mickleover
Derby DE3 9AJ
www.northbridgepublishing.co.uk
sales@northbridgepublishing.co.uk

A CIP catalogue record for this book is available from the
British Library.

ISBN 978-0-9926779-4-7

Book design by Graham Hales, Derby

Printed and bound by CMP (UK) Ltd, Dorset

Contents

Foreword

IT is almost 50 years since I first became aware of Mickleover, other than it being just a name on a map. I was working at the *Derby Evening Telegraph*'s district office at Burton upon Trent and usually travelled there from Derby aboard the Blue Bus Company's service that went via Findern, Willington and Repton. But sometimes, just for a change of scenery, I would catch the service that went through Etwall. And that, of course, meant travelling through Mickleover.

The bus still came up Burton Road, but then it swung down Chain Lane and Corden Avenue before turning on to Uttoxeter Road. And, very soon, it was in the heart of the old village of Mickleover. I often thought that one day I would like to live in Mickleover. In 1987, I managed it, and remain here today.

Of course, 50 years ago, Mickleover, while it might have been well on the way to becoming pretty much a suburb of Derby, still retained the feel of a village. That Blue Bus service boasted a driver and a conductor, and it would stop wherever anyone laden with shopping wanted to alight. Today's one-man-operated Trent buses probably aren't allowed to do that.

There were no supermarkets, not in Mickleover or anywhere else so far as I can recall. Small businesses and personal service was the order of the day. Happily, that is one thing that has not changed in half a century. Mickleover still has plenty of private enterprises where it is a delight to shop. Today, when people pop "into the village", they find a Mickleover both very much changed but also still vaguely reminiscent of a bygone age.

When I first bounced through here, on one of those Tailby & George Blue Buses, there were still more fields than streets, once you left the main road. Mickleover Golf Club had yet to be bisected by the bypass. Cyclists still obeyed the rules of the road, rang their bells, and never rode on pavements. There was no such thing as a video recorder, and therefore no such thing as a video shop. That such a shop came to Mickleover and has now disappeared again, illustrates just what changes have been wrought since the early 1960s.

The purpose of *It Happened In Mickleover* is to remind ourselves how things were "back in the day", as it is now fashionable to say. The book is not intended to be a definitive history of this place, but more a series of snapshots of the events and the people who made Mickleover the village it was from the mid-18th century to the mid-20th.

And telling it "how it was" through the words of local newspapers, the *Derby Mercury* as well as various Census returns and the *Derby Daily* (later *Evening*) *Telegraph*, brings those events and those people to life. From a sleepy rural backwater to a bustling village on the brink of becoming a busy suburb, the story of Mickleover over those 200 years from 1750 to 1960 is a fascinating one.

Anton Rippon
Mickleover
Spring, 2014

Acknowledgements

THIS book has been compiled by Nicola Rippon from the pages of the *Derby Evening Telegraph*, the *Derby Daily Telegraph* and the *Derby Mercury* as well as various Census returns and the Commonwealth War Graves Commission. Photographs have come from several sources, with many loaned to us by readers and from Bill Short's collection of postcards.

A Contented Village

"PAST the villas, and semi-detached villas of the Derby Gradgrings and Bounderbys [two wealthy employers in Charles Dickens's *Hard Times*] ... past the cemetery half-hidden by trees in the full beauty of their spring foliage ... past the barracks with its drill field trampled by military boots ... past the Small Pox Hospital ... past the site of the new Union ... past the smiling hedgerows from which the hawthorn is bursting into beauteous bloom ... past fields glowing in glorious wealth of the golden buttercups and the silver-tipped daisy ... past old-fashioned farms, and inviting green lanes. Past picturesque straw-thatched cottages, where the rich golden tassels of the laburnum gleam in the sunlight and the white and purple lilacs perfume the air. Past the contented little village of Mickleover ...'where health and plenty cheers the labouring swain' [a quote from *The Deserted Village* by Oliver Goldsmith] ... a sudden turn from the highway, and the tall towers of the Asylum end the pleasant perspective."

Description of the cab journey from Derby to Mickleover in the 1880s.

1

A Growing Village

THE name "Mickleover" comes from the Old English name "Michelovre" meaning "Great Ridge" and is first recorded in 1386. Prior to this the village is known as "Ufre" and "Ufram Majorem".

In early records Mickleover was the property of Morcar, who had been gifted it by Ethelred the Unready. At the Norman Conquest, William the Conqueror gave the land to Burton Abbey. The Manor of Mickleover belonged to the abbey until the Dissolution of the Monasteries by Henry VIII.

The Church of St Nicholas (now All Saints') was built in the centre of Mickleover in the 13th century on what was probably the shell of an older church. It was a time of great chaos, with the Plague spreading through town and countryside and, in Derby alone, one-third of the clergy fell victim. Although the land that "belonged" to the parish of Mickleover stretched as far as Burnaston, and a considerable way towards Derby, the census generally considered the linear extent to go from Bonehill Farm to Rough Heanor Farm and encompassing Huffin Heath.

The County Lunatic Asylum was within the boundaries of the village but was listed separately on the census. While staff and their families were listed in full, only their initials identified the patients.

EVEN though Mickleover was primarily a rural community, with a vast majority of inhabitants employed as agricultural labourers, a significant number of residents were flax spinners, some of whom might otherwise have descended into poverty. Other occupations included blacksmith and whitesmiths (who worked in lighter metals), a surprising number of bricklayers and several joiners. In outbuildings behind the Masons' Arms, lived Frederick Gregor, whose blacksmith's workshop was also located there. The workshops can clearly be seen on a map of 1882.

IN 1790, the *Derby Mercury* announced that a meeting would be held to discuss an Act of Parliament "intitled, Mickleover Inclosure – An Act for dividing and inclosing the Open Fields, Common Meadows and Pastured, Common and Waste Lands, in the Liberty or Lordship of Mickleover".

"Common" land was that considered to be available by a large group of people – somewhere residents could graze their animals and where crops could be grown. It was generally in the ownership of the lord of the manor, but rented out to individuals or families. "Waste" land was not officially claimed by any group and was often used by the poorer residents of a village. Inclosure, or Enclosure was of great significance in Britain since it really brought an end to common usage of land.

The meeting was held at the Nag's Head. Locals were warned that if they had any claims against the enclosure then they should attend that meeting or "they will from thenceforth be exclude and debarred of and from all Right and Title of and to the Lands to be inclosed".

IN the early 1840s, silk weavers' cottages were built along Common End (now Park Road) and in the very early 20th century, more housing was built along Western Road – then Poke Lane. In the 1930s, the remaining, generally smaller, properties were built in the spaces between the older houses. The area of Mickleover to the rear of Western Road, and featuring many Antipodean street names, was begun in the 1950s.

In 1872, the Water Works Company applied for permission to supply water to outlying areas of Derby, including Mickleover. Under law, the company was permitted to compulsorily purchase lands for filter tunnels and completion of the works.

~~~~~~~~~~~~~~~~~~~~~~~~~~~~~~~~

AS the village grew, occupations became more diverse and more industrial. The arrival of the railway brought with it related workers such as signalmen and railway clerks, porters and points men. As the 19th century drew to a close, several better-off Derby families moved out into what was fast becoming a distant suburb of the town. George Brigden, tailor and outfitter (whose family's shops still exist in the city centre) lived at The Gables on Station Road.

~~~~~~~~~~~~~~~~~~~~~~~~~~~~~~~~

PRIOR to the 20th century, street lighting in the village was all but non-existent. The Mickleover and Etwall Gas and Coke Company supplied gas. Their gasworks were situated along the Etwall Road, close to the current site of the Seven Wells pub.

But the establishment of even a few gaslights was an expensive business. In order to finance them, various fund-raising events were organised. These included a concert in December 1889, featuring performances by many locals as well as the County Asylum String Band and a guest singer from Derby, Miss Swindell. Two further concerts were held the following January. Eventually enough money was raised to install four gas lamps in the centre of the village. In 1912, the Council gave formal sanction to the Derby Corporation to obtain a provisional order authorising them to supply electric light at Mickleover. Universal electric street lighting was introduced into Mickleover in 1932. In 1909, the National Telephone Company had been permitted to erect 18 telegraph poles in the village.

~~~~~~

WITH Mickleover growing fast and modernisation gathering pace, the Mickleover Ratepayers' and Property Owners' Association was founded. In 1930, Honorary Secretary Mr F. S. Cowlishaw told the *Derby Evening Telegraph*: "We are very anxious to get all residents in Mickleover into the association." He said that the association had been set up "to get better terms from the County Council in the road-widening scheme near Chain Lane. I have invited residents of the village to join and all will be welcome."

In June 1930, under the headline "Residents Alarmed At Mickleover", the *Derby Evening Telegraph* reported that local residents of the Mickleover end of Chain Lane were concerned with the number of traffic accidents that were occurring in the thoroughfare. Privately owned motorcars were becoming more common and it was estimated that every Sunday during the summer months, hundreds of cars and cycles wound their

In the late 1930s an open-top car on its way to Mickleover shares Uttoxeter Road with horses and carts.

way down the lane from Burton Road to Uttoxeter Road and vice-versa. The majority of accidents were happening at the "dangerous S bend" a few hundred yards from the Uttoxeter Road end (between what are now the junctions with Muirfield Drive and Corden Avenue). Calls to widen the junction came to nothing, however. By 1935, the new Corden Avenue, which took traffic directly between Burton and Uttoxeter Roads was completed, leaving residents of the narrow part of Chain Lane in peace.

IN 1937, work began on widening Uttoxeter Road between the new City Hospital and the junction with Corden Avenue. To enable this, strips of land were to be removed from more than 100 of the new villa residences that had been built on that section of road. A line was to be cut through the banks that edged the road, and, after an appeal, householders were to have retaining walls built by the council, ensuring that what remained of the banks would not collapse.

IN the early 1930s visitors to Mickleover could have been forgiven for getting rather "turned around" when they tried to find their destination. With more than 1,000 houses in the village, there was still no system of numbering and most of the byways had no street name signs. This caused great problems for those not familiar with the village. "Mickleover Boy" wrote to the *Derby Evening Telegraph* describing the "adventures" of such visitors. "Tradesmen and others are put to endless inconvenience through the absence of numbers on house." He claimed to be "the 20th pedestrian stopped on Western Road by a visitor who was 'house hunting' and he was unable to give the necessary information".

A *Derby Evening Telegraph* correspondent declared it was "the easiest thing in the world to get lost at Mickleover".

Mickleover was described as "a maze of Smiths, nooks, cosy and otherwise, cottages galore of all descriptions, braes bonny and heather, and villas of all known brands".

"For Mickleover is that wonder suburb of Derby – the place where houses without numbers run riot in unnamed streets."

Just about every house, it seemed, had a name but no number.

"Mickleover may be described as a charming place by house agents, it may be an ideal suburb for its residents, but its streets are called something a great deal stronger than nameless by luckless strangers."

"Quite apart from this is the fact many houses carry the same designation, some of the terrace houses are not numbered, some of the semi-detached type have never been named, and names once painted on others have become so obliterated by weather conditions that they are undecipherable."

~~~~~~

STREET names in Mickleover have changed greatly over the years. Here are some old names and their modern-day equivalents.

Back Street – now Orchard Street

Nether Lodge Lane – the Hollow

Common End – Park Road

Cattle Hill, (previously Cackle Hill after the hill on which it stood) and Holy-End Street – now parts of Vicarage Road.

Derby Road – the section of Uttoxeter Road outside The Vine.

Fennel Street – Limes Avenue

Goosecroft Lane – the village end of Station Road

Poke Lane – Western Road from 1910 when locals decided that the old name "is a name of no value and led to nowhere of any importance".

Town Street – Etwall Road

~~~~~~

IN 1933, there was great turmoil when a plan was announced to build three shops on part of Chain Lane. Locals objected,

Cackle Hill, now part of Vicarage Road.

reminding the Council that the area had been declared "residential" by town planners; that the shops were simply not needed (the lane being only a mile or so from the shops of both Mickleover and Littleover); and that the value of the private homes would be diminished.

A representative of the builders, Derwent Builders Ltd, expressed his surprise that residents would consider that "such a convenience would be unwelcome". Indeed, several residents of Chain Lane wrote to the local paper declaring their support for the scheme and agreeing that having shops no nearer than a mile from home was a serious inconvenience.

IN 1975, the Mickleover Conservation Area was established. Encompassing the old centre of the village, it protects the area around All Saints' Church and Mickleover Manor, takes in part of the village end of Vicarage Road, part of Uttoxeter Road and Etwall Road and the area to the rear of the Square as well as part of The Hollow.

2

A Rural Community

IN September 1753, Sarah Beeson of Mickleover and Mr Richard Ward of Derby placed an advertisement in the *Derby Mercury*:

"Stoll'n or Stray'd on Sunday Night the 2nd of this Instant September, out of the Lanes adjoining to Mickleover near Derby A Light Bay MARE; About 14 Hands high, comes five Years old, Slouch Ear'd, mark'd on the Rump with an S with a Black Mane and Tail. Whoeover will give Intelligence of her, so that she may be had again … will receive Half a Guinea Reward, and reasonable Charges."

ON 13 April 1778, after "Pointer Dogs" had killed several sheep in the parish, the "principal Inhabitants of the Parish of Mickleover" placed an advertisement in the *Derby Mercury*. They announced it was their intention "to prosecute with the utmost Severity the Owner or Owners of any Dog or Dogs that may hereafter do any Damage by killing any Sheep or Lambs in the Parish of Mickleover".

WITH farmers being so central to the economies of villages like Mickleover, it seems that manufacturers were keen to use their testimonies to promote their goods. In 1779, a letter appeared on the front page of the *Derby Mercury*. It purported to be an unsolicited letter of thanks to "Mr Page of Breadsall" from Mickleover farmer, "John Gregory the younger.

It began:

"Sir, I think I should be undeserving the Benefit I have received, and greatly deficient in Gratitude, if I omitted informing you, that I am so far recovered from a dangerous CONSUMPTIVE CASE, by taking your Restorative Medicine that I was able to attend my Duty in the Field all the last Harvest. I had taken a great many Medicines from the faculty in the Counties of Derby and Leicester, before I made use of yours, but found no Relief till I sent for you, when after taking six Bottles, found myself little or no better, however by your second Attendance and Advice, I took two more Bottles, and in one Week, from that Time, found myself much better, and by taking six more Bottles am now perfectly recovered. I must therefore beg Leave to recommend it to those who may have Occasion for your valuable Medicine, not to be too hasty in leaving it off, but to give it a fair Trial, and I doubt not, but by the blessing of God they will find speedy and certain Relief."

For those persuaded to try the remedy, and to keep buying bottles until they were fully recovered, there was a note below the letter informing potential customers that "Mr Page may be spoke with every Friday at the Sign of the Seven Stars, near St Mary's Bridge, Derby."

Mr Page probably made quite a fortune with each bottle costing 6s. Mr Gregory spent more than £4 on his "cure" - the equivalent of more than £450 in modern terms.

IN 1786, "on Wednesday last as a Man was helping to make a Rick of Hay, at Mickleover near this Town, he unfortunately fell from the Top of a Cart, loaded, and pitching upon the back Part of his Head, was killed on the Spot".

IN a more rural age the "Killing of Game" was strictly restricted. Newspapers and periodicals published what they called a "Correct List (In Alphabetical Order) of the Certificates issued by the Clerk of the Peace for the County of Derby." In Mickleover only Samuel Rowland, who was in possession of a "Gentleman's Certificate", and the Reverend Benjamin Ward, who was granted a "Gamekeeper's Certificate", were permitted to hunt game.

IN 1837 the *Derby Telegraph* reported: "At the South Derbyshire Agricultural Society's Room, in this town, was exhibited by Mr Wade of Mickleover, a remarkably well grown Pomeranian Turnip, weighing 18lbs and measuring in circumference 37 inches. It had only one principal root and was nearly spherical. It was taken from a 3-acres close in the parish of Mickleover. The above weight does not include any of the foliage."

RURAL communities like Mickleover often played host to "ploughing matches". Huffin Heath Farm held such a competition on 4 October 1838: "The Ploughmen will assemble with their Teams at 9 o'clock in the morning, at the Plough Inn, near Mickleover, which is very near the Ground and will start precisely at 10 o'clock." Almost 60 years later, in 1895, the Derbyshire Agricultural Society's ploughing match was again being held at the same farm. This time there was also hedge-cutting and cattle-judging competitions.

Contemporary illustration of a 19th-century ploughing match at the White family's Rough Heanor Farm.

IN July 1843, there was much national press interest in an event held at Mickleover by the Royal Agricultural Society of England. The Society had been holding its annual show in Derby and the attendance of "practical farmers and gentlemen" was "exceedingly numerous". Many had come to see the raft of new machinery and devices that had been invented. A special trial was set up at White's Farm at Rough Heanor on "very stiff land". However, while many implements stood up well to the test, the ploughs were less successful. "Considerable dissatisfaction was expressed" and it was generally thought that, while the new ploughs would probably work adequately, they would not prove very useful on land like that on Mr White's farm. *The Spectator Magazine*, however, seemed to think it was the fault of the Mickleover soil and reported that a special meeting of the Society had been held at which the report from Derby was that no prizes had been awarded "for the ploughs best adapted to light or to heavy soils, because the soil used for the trial was of a mixed quality, not suited to bring forth the merits contemplated by the prizes".

IN late February 1847, the *Derby Mercury* reported that the people of Mickleover had generously collected money to be sent to "the distressed Irish and Scotch" who were suffering during the famine.

Amounts donated were as follows:

The Hon and Revd the Vicar	£5
Robert John Bell Esq	10s
Mr John Mold White	10s
Mr B. Hind	5s
Mr Ryley	2s 6d

IN 1847, the *Derby Mercury* published the following advertisement:

"Huffin Heath – Very superior Incalved and Barren Short-horned Cows, Heifers and Stirks" In addition, the farmer, Mr Hodgkinson, was selling a "Fat Bullock" a "Fat Calf", "three superior Colts and Waggon Mare, Porket and Store Pigs, Leicester Ewe and Tup Hogs, quantity of Wheat and Barley Straw (to be taken off the premises), Waggons, Carts, Ploughs etc and about Two Hundred Strike of Second Early and Seed Potatoes".

IN 1877, the *Derby Mercury* reported: "John Clarke, a youth, was summoned for being in the unlawful possession of a rabbit, at Mickleover, on the 26th of October. Police-sergeant Lees had found the defendant with a rabbit in his pocket. He said his uncle, who lived at Wilton, had given it to him, but this was found to be incorrect. Fined 5s and costs."

~~~~~~

IN 1879, the *Nottingham Evening Post* reported: "Swine Fever in Derbyshire – There have been fresh outbreaks of swine fever on the farms of William Garratt of Mickleover and William Morley of Littleover."

~~~~~~

IN December 1889, Mickleover lad Edward Pegge was summoned for ill-treating a pony in Curzon Street in Derby. He had been driving "an old bay pony attached to a milk cart. He had a short thick whipstick with him and he was beating the animal most unmercifully".

A witness, school board officer Mr Martin, "saw him strike it 35 times in a very short distance". An RSPCA officer gave evidence that, when he examined the animal shortly afterwards, "it showed signs of hard thrashing." Pegge told the court he had only hit it ten times and that he was "very sorry". He was fined 5s including costs.

~~~~~~

SOMETIMES the rural nature of the village leached into everyday life in the most unexpected ways. In July 1931, the *Derby Evening Telegraph* featured the headline: "Mickleover Cow Amok."

It seems that great excitement had been caused when a cow, being driven to a farm at Findern, had got loose. "The cow, after running along the road, dashed into a yard and garden, where it damaged produce and a wall. Later the animal went into the school yard."

The lone cow caused chaos: "People scattered in all directions."

The solution, however, was quite simple: "The cow was driven into a herd of other cows where it became quiet."

~~~~~~

MICKLEOVER – FIRST FOR CHEESE

RIGHT on the edge of Mickleover parish, in an area that modern residents might regard as bordering on Burnaston, one of the village's most surprising employers opened in the 1870s – the Mickleover cheese factory.

Lord Vernon of Sudbury had started an initiative among county landowners to establish such factories, which could be operated on something of a co-operative and which would utilise, and provide a steady market, for milk from local dairy farmers.

C. E. Newton, the owner of Mickleover Manor, initially began the manufacture on a smaller scale in a disused school room but, in 1874, a new purpose-built factory was erected and was capable of "dealing with the milk of 800 cows", all of which were farmed within a small geographical area. That year, among many newspapers across the country, the *Derby Mercury* published the "Practical Report of the Derbyshire Cheese Factories" by William Livesey of Preston and Edward Etches of Derby.

"Judging of the qualities of the cheese made at the respective factories, we had little difficulty in deciding to place Mickleover first. The method of making adopted there is … similar to that carried out by the best Somersetshire makers."

The factory was eventually sold to Brettles, makers of Stilton.

UNTIL the 1960s Nestlé had a sweet and biscuit factory on Station Road beside the railway station. Keiller also traded there. The site was taken over by Rolls-Royce for its training centre before being cleared and a new housing estate, centred on Whistlestop Close, erected

3

Transports of Delight

I N 1827, two regular coaches ran through Mickleover. On Mondays, Wednesdays and Fridays one travelled from Derby to Newcastle under Lyme, and on Tuesdays and Fridays another left Derby bound for Manchester.

IN 1865, *The Derby Mercury* published announcements from the Midland Railway of applications they intended to make to extend their network. This included "A Railway to commence in the township of Findern, in the parish of Mickleover ... by a junction with the main line of the Midland Railway at a point twenty-four chains or thereabouts to the southward of the bridge carrying that Railway over the Grand Trunk Canal ... which intended Railway will pass from, through or into several parishes, townships, and extra-parochial or other places following ... Findern, Mickleover, Sinfin Moor, Sinfin and Arlestone ..."

IN 1871, the *Derbyshire Times* revealed that it was the Great Northern Company that now wished to build a line through the area from Chaddesden and Spondon to Little Chester and Derby, to Mackworth, Markeaton, Mickleover and Radbourne.

AT the end of January 1878, the first goods and coal trains took to the rails of the new Great Northern line. By the following year, in addition to goods and passenger services, some special excursions operated along the line.

Milk churns from local farms stand on the snow-covered platform of Mickleover Station.

"Great Northern Railway – Cheap Excursions November 4th to LONDON from Egginton at 5.35 am, Etwall 5.38, Mickleover 5.45, Derby (Friar Gate) 5.50, West Hallam 6.00."

The next day another trip took passengers to Longsight (for Belle Vue Gardens in Gorton) and Manchester.

IN 1879, at a meeting to discuss mental health facilities, the rather prescient Alderman Cox from Derby spoke of "Derby spreading to Mickleover a few years hence, and the probability of tram cars running between the two places every ten minutes."

IN 1901, the *Derby Daily Telegraph* reported what may well have been the first motor-powered road traffic accident in the village. "A serious accident occurred to a motor-car near Mickleover … the car, which belonged to a Derby tradesman, had been utilised for delivering goods at Mickleover and was making the return journey when one of the tyres came off and caused the car to swerve and rush into the hedge. The driver and his companions were thrown out but escaped with a few bruises. The car, however, was overturned and the iron portion became ignited owing to the upsetting of the oil"

~~~~~~

IN 1871, the *Derby Mercury* reported: "Shortly before nine o'clock on Saturday night, as the driver of the mail cart between Uttoxeter and Derby was returning to Derby, after having left Mickleover, the cart was run into by a light trap, in which were two or three men. The driver of the mail cart was thrown out, the shafts were broken, and the harness was injured. The occupants of the other conveyance drove off, however, and their names have not been ascertained."

~~~~~~

THE railway aside, public transport was something rather lacking where Mickleover was concerned.

In 1907, the *Derby Daily Telegraph* reported: "Derby Tramways Committee and the Uttoxeter Road Route – Important Recommendation."

There had been, it seemed, some debate as to the proposed position of the terminus of the "Uttoxeter Road electric car route". Originally this was expected to be at the corner of Albany Road. Some householders had complained and a new proposal suggested it be placed 70 yards nearer the town. This was widely felt to be far too near Derby and a suggestion was made that it be sited at the corner of Constable Lane, some 459 yards further out than Albany Road and approximately level with the present city end of the Royal Derby Hospital. If the terminus were sited there "there is a good chance of catering for the inhabitants of Mickleover, many of whom would have little further to walk to Constable Lane only a mile and a half to the edge of the village than to the Great Northern Railway Station which was a mile and a quarter from the village.

~~~~~~

IN June 1924, an Alvaston man had a lucky escape when his aeroplane crashed in Radbourne Lane. An eyewitness reported that the plane "swooped over a field of mowing grass, skinned the top of the hedge skirting the road, and nosed into a dry ditch on the other side of the road". The aeroplane was badly damaged and "rendered temporarily useless". The pilot was unhurt.

The *Derby Daily Telegraph* reported: "The disabled machine, in crashing, left just sufficient space for traffic to pass along the lane."

~~~~~~

BY 1930, public transport to Mickleover had improved somewhat, but still attracted criticism from visitors. In a letter to the *Derby Daily Telegraph* "Only A Visitor" complained at the number of stops the bus to Mickleover had to make. "Every householder or passenger expected to be dropped or picked up right upon the doorstep or gateway. Just imagine the energy required to stop a crowded bus about 24 to 30 times than less than half a mile."

The correspondent asked: "Could it not be arranged that regular stopping places be made by the residents and not so haphazard as now? I am sure that someone would be grateful for this, and what a saving there would be in wear and tear of brake linings etc."

~~~~~~

IN August 1931 an omnibus travelling between Mickleover and Derby ran into a ditch on Western Road. Damage to the bus was not serious, but it was unable to continue its journey and passengers had to be transferred to another vehicle.

~~~~~~

Chain Lane c.1924, in the days before the laying of Corden Avenue, when this really was a country lane.

IN February 1932, the *Derby Evening Telegraph* reported that a "new omnibus war has started". Mickleover's Property Owners' and Ratepayers' Association wrote to the East Midland Traffic Commissioners to complain about Derby Corporation's application to run buses along Uttoxeter Road as far as Western Road in Mickleover. In 1931, Parliament had fixed the junction of Chain Lane and Uttoxeter Road as the boundary beyond which the Corporation could not run services, leaving this area to be served by private firms. There were real fears that the Corporation was trying to poach customers from those private firms.

BY 1938, the build-up of motor traffic was causing difficulties in Mickleover. Speeding traffic "moving through the village at 45 mph" and the lack of any kind of pedestrian crossing made it dangerous for pedestrians, according to a meeting of the Mickleover Property Owners' and Ratepayers' Association. The County Council was to be asked for such a crossing and for the erection of a "Halt" sign at the end of Chain Lane near the Corden Avenue junction.

4

Handsome Properties

MICKLEOVER has long been a popular place to live. In 1755, the *Derby Mercury* advertised: "A large new-built, handsome brick HOUSE standing in Mickleover … containing three Rooms on a Floor, with a Pantry and Closets; the best Rooms being Sash'd; Also a Brewhouse, with room for two Coppers and a good Oven; three Cellars, and a Pantry adjoining; with Lead Pipes and Cisterns for catching Rain Water and many other Conveniences. Also three Gardens, and planted with the choicest Wall Fruit; a large Barn Yard, two large Barns, a Stable, Hove etc, fit either for a Gentleman or a substantial Farmer. There is also five Acres and a Half of good Grass Ground and four Acres and a Half of Plough Land, to be sold with the above House. There is also to be sold, about Three Acres of good Grass Ground, lying near the said House, and one Acre of Plough Land in the Mill Field. Likewise, two new Brick Dwelling Conveniences thereto belonging, well tenanted. For further Particulars enquire of Mr John Wright junior, Attorney at Law in Derby, or Mr John Woollatt at Mickleover."

1775 *Derby Mercury*
"A Freehold Messuage, with the Garden (walled around), Yard, Barn, Stable and other convenient Out-Houses, situate in

Mickleover, 3 Miles from Derby, adjoining the Turnpike Road leading from Derby to Uttoxeter, and late in the Possession of Mrs Warde.

Also a TENEMENT standing near to the said Messuage, with the Barn and Garden thereto belonging, now in the Tenure of William Yeomans.

N.B. There is a right of Common belonging to the said Premises, which is very extensive, and when inclosed will be of great Advantage to the same."

1834 *Derby Mercury*
"By Mr Titterton. Valuable FREEHOLD PROPERTY in MICKLEOVER, near Derby
TO BE SOLD BY AUCTION
At the House of Mr Thomas Pywell, the Old Plough Inn, at Huffenheath, near Mickleover …

Lot 1 … all that Close of excellent Old Turf Land, situate in Mickleover aforesaid, called the Windmill Piece …

Lot 2 … All that valuable Piece of LAND, also situate in Mickleover aforesaid, called the Field Close … "

1838 *Derby Mercury*
"Mickleover House … elegant modern furniture, Plate, Books, Kitchen Requisites, Brewing Vessels, Grand Piano Forte, Patent Mangle &c &c … to be sold by Auction … on the Premises of the late ROBERT DELL Esq at Mickleover … the Dining, Drawing, and Library Furniture comprises a set of solid Spanish mahogany telescope dining tables with reeded legs on castors … rich Bengal carpet … beautiful French time-piece … Three fat Scotch bullocks, incalf cow, useful hackney and harness mare, store pig, stack of well got hay, hives of bees …"

The same property was again for sale in 1896. This advertisement in the *Derby Mercury* detailed that the sale also offered "Lodge at Entrance containing four rooms and storage rooms, Gardener's Cottage with four rooms and attics. Adjoining is a well arranged set of Farm Buildings"

AT a sale in 1841, announced in the *Derby Mercury*, a number of properties were for sale. Included among them were "a well-built and respectable Residence ... adapted either for a farm house or private family, with excellent outbuildings ... two Closes of Land, forming part of the Gorsey Closes, called Near Gorsey and Gorsey Meadow, with an excellent frontage to the road leading from Mickleover to Ashbourne ... all that Close of very rich Pasture Land, commonly called Pingle or Water Fallow ... "

IVY House, as we see it today, was built the 1820s. However, in the cellar is a stone carved with the initials "G W 1694".

Ivy House, once the home of the Wade family.

SOME Mickleover properties were so impressive that their sale was advertised far and wide. In 1846, the *Royal Leamington*

The Limes, once home to the Ayre family, now serves
as a residential home for the elderly.

Courier featured an advertisement for "That Most Beautiful
Villa Residence, called The Limes".

The house had "only been erected about five years" and of
particular interest were the "Pleasure, Flower and Vegetable
Gardens". Rooms are described as "lofty, spacious, and elegant,
commanding a delightful and extensive South-West view of the
surrounding neighbourhood."

Features included "China Closet ... Butler's Pantry ...
Brewhouse, Ale and Wine Cellars ... Carriage House and
Harness Room... two Stall Stable, Cowshed, Dairy and Larder,
Waggon and Cart Sheds, Piggery ... genteel Cottage with Coach
House".

The "Flower Garden, Lawn and Plantation" were "most
tastefully laid out" and the "Vegetable Gardens are in a high state
of cultivation, with a variety of bearing Fruit Trees, Vinery &c".

In 1897, the *Derby Daily Telegraph* reported: "Mr and Mrs
Ayre, of The Lymes, recently entertained their tenants' wives

The rear aspect of The Limes is clearly visible from roads south of the village.

and families, when upwards of 40 responded to the invitation. Each wife received the acceptable present of a warm striped rug, and each child useful garments, toys, sweets and nuts, which testified to the thoughtful care of the donors. Afterwards they were thoroughly regaled with a plentiful supply of good things, and games were thoroughly enjoyed. Hearty cheers for Mr and Mrs Ayre brought a very pleasant evening to a close."

1891, *Derby Mercury*
"Valuable Freehold Dwelling-House with Blacksmith's Forge, Workshops, Stabling, and Building Land, Fronting to the Square, and the Green."

IN 1904 it was announced in the *Derby Daily Telegraph* that two houses were being erected in Poke Lane "for the reception and care of disabled soldiers" formerly with the Sherwood

Foresters. In August that year it was further reported that two such houses – "exceedingly nice cottages" – had been built in North Avenue "to be used by men of the Notts and Derbyshire Regiment who through wounds received in the South African war are incapacitated from doing any work except that of the very lightest nature".

North Avenue, once a leafy avenue lined with grass verges.

The cottages had bay windows and were described as being "pleasantly situated".

"In a prominent place in front of the two cottages is the crest of the regiment in stone". Inside an inscription read: "These cottages were erected in memory of HRH Prince Christian Victor of Schleswig-Holstein who died for his Queen and country, South Africa 1900."

The first men to occupy the homes were Sergeant Sargent and Private Fletcher and their families.

Both men had been severely injured during the Boer War. Sergeant Sargent had had a leg amputated and Private Fletcher had endured "very bad" wounds to his legs.

THE Old Hall, on Orchard Street and once called The Cedars, has a carving over the door: "Nisi Deus Frustra 1648." The precise meaning of the translation from Latin is open to varied interpretations but is thought to refer to a psalm, the essence of which means: "Without God, there is frustration."

Its first owners, the Cotchett family, were supporters of the Commonwealth during the English Civil War and legend tells that Oliver Cromwell himself, or at least one of his officers, spent the night there.

THE house that straddles the corner of Orchard Street, then Back Street, and Etwall Road, opposite All Saints', was once home to Smith's Tea Rooms. Run by asylum attendant Jonathan Smith and his wife Jane, it remained open until 1910.

Members of the Smith family stand outside their tearooms on the corner of Orchard Street and Etwall Road in the early 1900s.

NOT all living arrangements in Mickleover were of the highest quality. In July 1931 the *Derby Daily Telegraph* reported that Jack Lees, MP for Belper, had asked the Minister of Health, in the House of Commons, how many houses in Mickleover "had been declared unfit for human habitation". The minister, Mr Greenwood, replied that he believed that only one demolition order had been made and that Repton Rural Council intended to build 12 new houses in the village. Greenwood also said that "if you will give me the particulars" he would consider Mr Lees allegations that "there is a considerable amount of overcrowding in houses in this area".

MICKLEOVER'S LISTED BUILDINGS

All Saints' Church, Etwall Road (14th-century)

Mickleover Manor (1852)

Nos 13 to 18 The Green (early 19th-century)

Nos 1 and 2 The Hollow late (18th-century and early 19th-century)

No 4 The Hollow (16th or 17th-century)

Nos 5/6, No 7 and No 8 – The Hollow (19th-century)

11 Limes Avenue (18th-century)

The Limes, Limes Avenue (early 19th-century)

Old Hall, 5 Orchard Street (1649)

Gate piers at No 5 separately listed (17th-century)

4 and 5 The Square (The Gables) (17th-century or 18th-century)

Manor Farmhouse, 11 Vicarage Road (late 18th-century or early 19th-century)

Limes Avenue, originally known as Fennel Street, was once lined with a neat row of workers' cottages.

5

"Headquarters of the county imbeciles"

THE establishment of the County Lunatic Asylum was to have a huge impact on the village of Mickleover, both in terms of its physical growth, its nature, and upon the perception of the village on those from outside the area.

In 1851, the Derbyshire Pauper's Lunatic Asylum opened on an eight-acre site on the edge of Mickleover. Previously, private establishments like Green Hill House in Derby had treated its residents as inmates to be contained, with poor and harsh conditions commonplace. Mickleover was different. It was a pioneering establishment that regarded its residents as patients to be treated. The grounds featured beautiful landscaped gardens and a hospital farm as well as workshops. During its early years the Asylum received visitors from across Europe who wanted to model their own institutions upon it. However, by today's standards the public and, in particular, the press were less than understanding of the plight of those treated there. And they were certainly far from sensitive in their descriptions, calling the place the "Derbyshire Bedlam", for example.

The architect of the new Asylum was Henry Duesbury. In *A History and Directory of Derby* of 1849, Stephen Glover described

The Derbyshire Paupers' Lunatic Asylum sat on an 8-acre site featuring a farm, workshops and ornamental grounds.

the institution thus: "The wards or residences of the patients ... are placed in the best position facing the south, and overlooking the beautiful valley of the Trent, and the distant hills of three adjoining counties."

Of course, the very existence of an asylum to treat the mentally ill had its own complications. There were many sad cases and many tragic reasons why an individual might be sent there. And many of those treated at the Asylum simply did not want to be there. In January 1863 the *Derby Mercury* reported "INGENIOUS ESCAPE AND CLEVER CAPTURE OF A LUNATIC"

Jesse Stevenson, in a previous life a milk seller in Derby, had "fastened together a number of towels, by which he let himself down from a window in an upper storey, and silently wending his way across the grounds, scaled the wall at a convenient place, and thus effected his escape".

However, Stevenson's freedom was short-lived. Only half an hour after he left the asylum, he was spotted by Sergeant Shaw, the local police officer who "suspecting he was not altogether right from his peculiar demeanour, watched his movements".

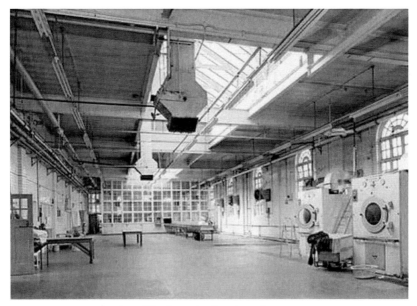

The huge Asylum laundry.

Stevenson apparently let forth a colourful list of threats against those in charge of the asylum. Troubled by this and "other visible signs of insanity", the sergeant took hold of Stevenson and "handed him over to attendants … who conveyed him back to his old quarters".

The Lunatic Asylum was noted for its kind treatments as well as for its social activities and involvement in the local village community. A brass band from the asylum played at many village celebrations. In January 1867, the *Derby Mercury* detailed the Christmas celebrations that had just passed. In a feature entitled "Christmas Eve at the Lunatic Asylum", the newspaper complimented those in charge for their efforts: "We know of no place where the enjoyment of Christmas is so cleverly ensured as the Mickleover Asylum. There, at any rate, are no failures. The managers know as well as any professional caterer how to make the best of the materials at their disposal, and somehow or other these materials invariably happen to be of a very superior calibre."

Dr Hitchman, who was in charge of the Asylum, organised very detailed, busy entertainment schedules for patients, staff and visitors alike. Everyone seemed "to enter well into the spirit of this desire, and flinging rank, prejudices, and all small-mindedness aside, rollicking fun, good music, and chatty communities are the ingredients of the happiness of Christmas Eve at the Mickleover Asylum".

The Asylum featured its own theatre in which all manner of entertainment was offered, most of which were "of a very original and striking character".

There was both comedy and drama, with a scene from William Shakespeare's *Julius Caesar* being performed, followed by a farce entitled *Nursery Chickweed*.

"Every part in the piece was represented with a fidelity and a sustained appreciation of character most remarkable in a band of amateurs."

It seemed that Asylum productions had quite a reputation for the quality of the acting "but then actors have been changed, and the managers must have a secret hoard of talent from which they can cull their favourites at pleasure". The theatrical performances were followed by music and games and dancing.

Particularly notable was a "splendid drop scene, representing a view of the exterior of the Asylum, painted by Mr Cantrill of Derby".

In February 1875 "our special commissioner", writing under the name "A Bohemian", wrote for the *Derbyshire Times* about a visit he had made to the Asylum. Not, it would seem, without a good deal of hesitancy:

"It requires a considerable amount of moral courage to deliberately hail a cabman and bid him drive to Mickleover." He need not have worried, for the cabman ignored his attempt at diplomacy. "Dr Lindsay's, the County Asylum? Right you are, Sir!" And a promise that "if there was one horse in Derby that could make brief business of the four miles between me and the Asylum, his was the animal".

The writer was somewhat surprised at the appearance of the building: "There is certainly nothing in the architectural appearance of the Asylum, with its splendid situation, its spacious lawn, its broad, gravelled walks, its conservatories, its lofty towers, its bow windows, and its noble entrance hall, to suggest that you are in the precincts of a mad house – where some hundreds of men and women, bereft of reason, and unaccountable for their actions are shut away from their fellows."

It was, he wrote, more like a "stately pile' or a "lordly mansion" and a unknowing visitor might covet "a niche in it where he could spend his leisure after the day's toil was over, and smell the fragrant flowers, and catch the health inspiring breath of the country".

The writer took some time to put the minds of readers at rest. Asylums were no longer the terrible places of "coercion, punishment and confinement" of the past. He noted that, despite this, "the multitude still regard a County Asylum, as the dread Bluebeard's cupboard of the neighbourhood".

It would, he noted, "tend to remove their erroneous impressions if such institutions as Mickleover were more frequently visited by the lower classes".

The accommodation, he wrote, was of the highest quality "lofty corridors, bright with sunshine and pictures, through long cheerful wards where mad men and mad women were surrounded with every comfort, and past rows of snug bedrooms characterised by the same exquisite cleanliness, airiness, cheeriness and order".

"Flowers and ferns were to be found everywhere. The walls were crowded with cheerful pictures. In more than one room was an aviary full of joyously caroling songsters, in others there were complete aquariums in which beautiful gold and silver

The Asylum boiler house.

fish glided among graceful water plants and under the arches of miniature grottos."

On one ward there was even a caged monkey, and newspapers and magazines were available on every ward.

"Music, chess, cards, bagatelle etc are provided for the amusement of the patients for these, with suavity, patience and tenderness have proved to be the best doctors."

The patients also seemed so much less "mad" than the writer had expected. "All the stages of lunacy that lie between wild fury and chronic dementia are, in the popular mind, merged in the raving maniac … Truth to tell I was the noisiest individual in the room."

However, further into the asylum, in the wards treating the "most mentally degraded types of humanity", things were a little starker. Patients bombarded the writer, and his doctor guide, with "questions and entreaties, all bewildered, incoherent and absurd. Some paced the rooms with scowling eyes and dishevelled hair, and with faces wild with anger and agony. Others addressed me as their lovers and husbands, and seemed inclined to exhibit endearments of a still tender character ... the most pathetic sights were afforded by the epileptic and imbecile patients. With the mind ruined and the nerve power destroyed, death would be to them welcome ... "

The former Asylum and its grounds are now known as Mickleover Country Park, a residential development with a thriving social club.

But even here, where the most wretched cases resided, "nothing strikes the visitor with greater admiration than the care taken of these utterly helpless creatures".

Many of the male patients were active in the workshops and in the grounds. "Occupation diverts the mind from its malady," Dr Watts told the writer.

In the workshops, men made clothes and shoes and did carpentry.

In May that year, the same writer reported on a theatrical performance held at the Mickleover Asylum at, what the writer calling it "An Evening At The Mickleover Theatre Royal".

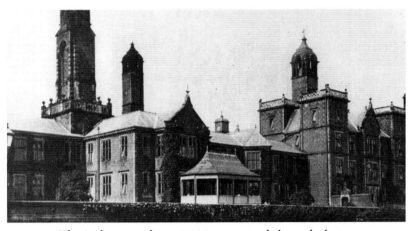

The Asylum, seen here c.1900, was extended greatly during its use as a mental hospital.

By 1879, it had become clear to those in power in Derby that a new Lunatic Asylum for the Borough alone was needed. Because the Mickleover institution was confined to those outside the Borough, Derby's "lunatics" had to be sent to an asylum in Leicester.

But this was controversial and the patients themselves drew little sympathy in some quarters. Writing in a less than sympathetic tone in the *Nottingham Post*, the "Derby Gossip" mocked the authority's attempts: "Lunatics exist and they are increasing at an alarming rate."

The possibility of combining with the County Asylum at Mickleover had been rejected and, instead, a new institution was to be erected on the Rowditch estate. When one alderman noted that the settlements of Derby and Mickleover grew ever closer, "Derby Gossip" seemed rather taken aback: "Just as though Derby folks would have any special inclination to extend the borough to Mickleover. What do we want near an Asylum?" He went on to describe Mickleover as "the headquarters of the county imbeciles".

In the end, the people of Derby did have the benefit of their own asylum – not far from Mickleover as it turned out.

6

Reasons to Celebrate

LIKE any thriving village, Mickleover held many fetes, galas and feasts. From Royal events to the agricultural year, all manner of events were cause for community celebration, even something as everyday as the birth of a baby to a local family. Mickleover celebrated its Winter Wakes on 6 December – St Nicholas' Day.

In late June 1857, a week of celebration of the birth of a son and heir to C. E. Newton Esq of Mickleover Manor. Festivities began with a "sumptuous repast consisting of good old English fare, together with every delicacy of the season" which was "provided and partaken of with great gusto" at the schoolroom. The room was "most tastefully decorated with evergreens".

Toasts, to Queen Victoria and the health of the Newtons and their infant son, were followed by further toasts to the well-being of some of the special guests from other local estates, and finally to that of the farmers and labourers. Wines and punch, the report in the *Derby Mercury* stated, "were of first class quality and one of the most happy meetings ever witnessed in Mickleover was kept up until 10 o'clock". A few days later "the greatest juvenile fete which has taken place in Mickleover within the memory of that remarkable personage 'the oldest inhabitant', was held on the beautiful grounds of the Manor House".

Treats were given to 150 children from the Day and Sunday schools, together with the wives, daughters and friends of the tenants of the estate. "A very short time elapsed before piles of rich plum cake and the apparently endless supplies of tea had suffered a visible decrease." The Asylum Brass Band provided entertainment. The greenhouse at Mickleover House, threw open its doors "for inspection". While the children went out on to the lawn to play the games that had been organized for them, some 60 adults partook of their own "excellent tea". After the games were done, there was dancing and the opportunity to tour the gardens and view the fine plants exhibited there.

ON New Year's Eve 1908, the Newtons again celebrated with the village, this time with a more formal ball to celebrate the coming-of-age of Rosamund Newton, the eldest daughter of Mr F. C. Newton and his wife. More than 200 tenants, neighbours and friends were invited to a ball at Mickleover Manor. Revellers danced to the music of a string band, and supper was provided midway through proceedings. The tenants presented Miss Newton with a "beautiful silver inkstand" as a testament to the "good feeling that existed between the tenants and Mr Newton and to the high esteem in which they held him and his family".

ROYAL celebrations were often marked in the village. In May 1935, a tea to celebrate the silver jubilee of King George V and Queen Mary was held in the Parish Hut. Each child attending was presented with a souvenir mug and a packet of sweets. A sports day for the children was held on the village playing field, while widows, widowers, unemployed villagers and old-age pensioners were served tea at the Council School, after which Mr Cross treated them to a cinema exhibition.

7

Places of Worship

ALL SAINTS' Church in Etwall Road was originally dedicated to St Nicholas. Much of the present building was erected in the early 14th century.

The font at All Saints' Church dates from the 14th century, but for several years it was used as an ornament in a neighbouring garden before being returned to its proper use.

All Saints' clock has only two faces, for those looking from the south and west. When it was installed there were only fields to the north and east.

~~~~~~~~~~~~~~~~~~~~~~~~~~~~~~

IN 1830, the *Derby Mercury* gave readers a review of, of all things, a church service: "On Sunday last an impressive sermon was preached in Mickleover Church, by the Revd John Leigh, Rector of Eggington, in aid of the Sunday Schools … a selection of sacred music was at the same sung by a part of the Derby Choral Society. Mr Ford's *Waft her Angels* etc by Handel was beautifully executed. The trio by Messrs Longman and Hawkridge and Miss England, from the opera of *Judah* was exquisite, and the chorus that followed well maintained … the chants were well given, perhaps a little too quick. The whole, however, was a charming and well-conducted performance. The Church was crowded, and the exertions both of the eloquent

Preacher, and of the Choral Society, were well rewarded by the handsome and liberal collection of £15 12s 6d."

IN November 1859, the *Derby Mercury* commented: "Another restoration has preserved to Derbyshire another architectural beauty, of which the county should be proud. Mickleover Church, dedicated to All Saints' fourteen hundred years ago, has many interesting associations clinging around its history, which are well worth the labour of those who are inclined to study them. Once the property of that daring, if not happy, Mercian monarch whose throne was rudely smashed at Repton, in after years it was handed over by William the Conqueror to the monastic rulers at Burton, and the old building passed through many storms, historical as well as elemental, till the years 1767, when it was partially destroyed by fire. The building that has just been restored at the cost of sixteen hundred pounds is, therefore, not an ordinary one, and the labour by which it has been strengthened and embellished has been a labour of love.

"With the spreading necessities of the age, the space has been enlarged, and more room is now at the disposal of God's

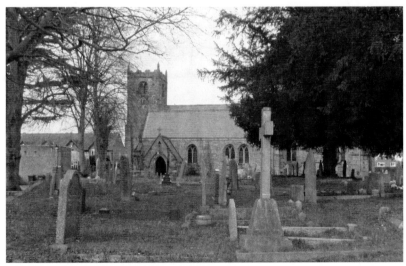

All Saints' Church, which was restored in 1859, and its large village graveyard.

worshippers. For a long time this grey old church, covered with the time-marking ivy, has been in a very dilapidated state. It now looks strong and well proportioned, but at the same time preserves some of its enduring marks of age.

"The old fashioned pews have given way to the more modern, if not more comfortable, seats now used pretty generally whenever restorations are effected. The north aisle has been enlarged, and besides the one hundred free sittings here open to all, there are two hundred and fifty others. The entrance porch is new, as is also the roof, and many parts of the interior alterations were necessitate not more by the ravages of time than the demand for more room. In the chancel a beautifully painted window, the gift of the vicar, has been put up. It is illustrative of the 25th chapter of the St Matthew, including the emblems of Faith, Hope and Charity … the floor inside the communion rail is exceedingly novel and beautiful … it is as effective as it is curious …"

In November 1895 the Suffragen Bishop of Derby dedicated a new church clock at All Saints'.

One of two clock faces on the tower of All Saints'.

ON 25 March 1914, on what the *Derby Daily Telegraph* described as "a bright, sunny afternoon", 12 foundation stones of the new Mickleover Wesleyan Chapel on Station Road were laid. Replacing a building that the church had been using for almost 100 years, it was expected to cost nearly £1,500 and the church was well on the way to raising the money, with donations from locals and others already reaching £553. Several local notables

The congregation of Mickleover Methodist Chapel gathers
to celebrate the completion of the new building in 1914.

each laid a stone, among them Miss Sharpe, who represented Mickleover Sunday School, and Councillor H. J. Bonas. One of those invited to lay a stone, Mrs Clower, told those in attendance that "she was once visiting a building when she saw on the walls the text: 'God helps those who help themselves'. The building in question was the workhouse". Her comments raised much laughter. She was, however, she assured her audience, certain that the people of Mickleover "did help themselves" and that "they would have all the encouragement they deserved".

By September 1914, the chapel was ready to hold its first services. Designed to seat 250 chapelgoers, it featured a vestry, a large schoolroom, a kitchen and lavatories. Ventilated by "natural means", heated by "the low pressure hot water system" and lit by "incandescent gas", it was a modern and comfortable building.

~~~~~~

IN October 1937 the Derby *Evening Telegraph* reported the dramatic news that, at a meeting of the Mickleover Parish Council, allegations had been made that graves in the parish churchyard had been "levelled-up" and used again for burials. Another suggestion was that gravestones that had partly fallen down had been "removed and stood against a wall". Mr J. Warner declared that this had happened three or four times to his knowledge and that it was "a public scandal". These claims were made as evidence that the village needed a public burial ground, since the churchyard was becoming filled.

Graves in All Saints' churchyard.

8

Some Notable Mickleover Residents

IN 1649, Mickleover man Robert Cotchett, of the The Cedars, also known as the Old Manor, was an observer at the execution of Charles I in Whitehall.

Silk weaving fascinated Robert Cotchett's son, Thomas. In 1704, he built a silk mill on the banks of the Derwent in Derby. Unfortunately, the Dutch machinery that Cotchett installed was not sophisticated enough to produce silk fine enough to rival that produced in Northern Italy. One of his employees, John Lombe, committed industrial espionage in Piedmont, bringing back to Derbyshire, in bales of imported silk, the secrets of Piedmontese silk. Lombe set up a factory next to Cotchett's old mill and this became the world's first factory – Derby's Silk Mill.

~~~~~~

THE Reverend Frederick Curzon was Vicar of All Saints' and quite a character. He was an illegitimate son of Nathaniel Curzon of Kedleston Hall and had been expelled from both Oxford and Cambridge Universities. He ran up large gambling debts, which were generally paid off by his mother. In 1821 he had a rather grand vicarage built at the top of Cattle Hill (now Vicarage Road). A known drinker, he was left out of the will of his wealthy wife and was known to be in the habit of neglecting to pay his servants.

THE *Derby Mercury* of 11 December 1867 reported the funeral of a veteran of the Crimean War. A former Grenadier Guardsman, the man was named in the newspaper only as "Webster". He had been a soldier for ten years and "was in the possession of several decorations", although he received no pension. Webster's cortege received quite a reception.

"The body was met at the entrance of the village by Major Newton, the drum and fife band, the firing party, and some 30 or 40 members of the Derby Companies … the procession … moved on at slow time, the drum and fife band playing the *Dead March* in *Saul*. The scene was an impressive one, as the cortege entered the churchyard amidst crowds of villagers, from many of whom sighs and suppressed sobs were heard."

Webster left a widow and two young children and the *Mercury* noted that it would be happy to "receive and acknowledge any subscription, however small" that readers may wish to donate to his grieving family.

AN 1872 directory lists Lieutenant-Colonel John Augustus Conolly VC as a resident of Mickleover. Lieutenant-Colonel Conolly, who was born in Ireland in May 1829, was serving with the 49th Regiment (later the Royal Berkshire Regiment – Princess Charlotte of Wales's) in the Crimean War when, on 26 October 1854, as a 25-year-old lieutenant, he led an attack on a Russian position at Sebastopol,

Lieutenant-Colonel John Augustus Conolly VC, Mickleover resident and hero of the Crimean War.

during which he was "dangerously wounded" and for which he was awarded the Victoria Cross: "Throwing off his grey greatcoat that all might distinguish him from the enemy, he flung himself on a party of Russians and cut one man down with his sword ... "

After the action he transferred to the Coldstream Guards. From 1872 to 1875, Conolly was adjutant to the 1st Derbyshire Militia. After leaving the Army he was appointed Sub-Commissioner for the Dublin Metropolitan Police and later Resident Magistrate for the Curragh of Kildare, where he died in December 1888.

IN July 1908 the *Derby Daily Telegraph* reported that there had been "Impressive scenes at Mickleover" as the village laid to rest Charles Edmund Newton of Mickleover Manor. He was widely regarded as generous and kind and "greatly beloved in the village", and Mickleover wore "an appearance of general mourning ... blinds drawn and work stopped".

IN March 1924 Matilda Ryley of Green Hill, Mickleover, passed away. Her death marked something of the end of an era, since the old lady was approaching 96 years old and was described in the *Derby Daily Telegraph* as Mickleover's "Oldest Inhabitant". She was the daughter of George Wade of Ivy House. She had been born and bred in the village. She had married Thomas Ryley of Brookfield Farm 70 years earlier and had been a widow for the last 25 years. "She was blessed, almost to the end, with a wonderful eyesight which she utilised, even as a nonagenarian, in painting in water colours. Her work, whether on silk or paper, was characterised by great artistic merit and fidelity to nature." Many cherished her work, and at least two pieces were given to Mickleover Golf Club.

ANOTHER death that was granted with a write-up in the local newspaper was that of John Campbell, an 87-year-old former gardener and weather expert. He had found work, at the age of 20, at Chatsworth House as a gardener and later worked as steward to the Newtons at Mickleover Manor. He had received prizes "at all the principal shows" for his horticulture and had become such an expert on weather that he advised, among others, the Air Ministry.

IN January 1946, one Mickleover publican found himself with a new job. Stuart McMillan, landlord of the Nag's Head Hotel, was appointed the new manager of Derby County Football Club. McMillan had enjoyed a successful professional sporting career of his own, having played for the Rams, as well as for Wolverhampton Wanderers, Chelsea and Bradford City, and represented Derbyshire at cricket. He was also a talented golfer and billiards player. It would be quite an appointment. Three months later, McMillan oversaw the Rams' first –

Stuart McMillan, the Mickleover publican who became an FA Cup winning Rams manager.

and so far only – FA Cup Final victory. He remained manager of Derby County until 1953.

9
Lessons Learned

THE first formal school in Mickleover was held at All Saints' Church before, in 1784, Robert Newton gave £200 to establish a purpose-built school on The Green.

The *Derby Mercury* of 15 March 1787 carried the following advertisement: "Wanted At Mickleover near Derby A SCHOOL-MASTER, who writes a good Hand, understands Arithmetic, and is able to teach English grammatically. Candidates offering themselves to be examined on Monday in Whitsun Week.

Certificates of their Characters, attested by the Minister and other respectable Persons, to be sent (Post-paid) to the CHURCH-WARDEN of Mickleover, on or before Easter Week.

N.B. A School might answer well to a Person of Credit and Abilities, as Mickleover is a populous Village."

IN 1789 the *Derby Mercury* reported: "Mickleover Free-School, J & S Herris, Return sincere Thanks to all their Friends who have entrusted them with the Education of their Children and hope to merit a Continuance of the many invaluable Favours they had received; and their Friends and others who wish to honour them with the Care and Tuition of their Children, may be assured that their Pupils' Health, Morals, and Improvement, are their peculiar Study, and their utmost Endeavours will be exerted to give general Satisfaction. "They have Conveniencey for a few more Boarders, but no one can be admitted for a less Time than one Year. The School opens after the present Vacation on the 11th of January, 1790. Terms as usual.

N.B. Mickleover is a remarkable pleasant and healthful Situation, within three Miles of Derby."

IN 1852 the Newtons again helped out. A school to cater for 100 children was established in Orchard Street. Education was open to all children, at a small cost of 1d per week, although nine poor pupils were educated for free. This building later became the Coffee and Reading Room and is now a private house.

IN 1867, George Wade, of Mickleover Lodge (a property which is now within the grounds of Our Lady of Lourdes), gave some land to the people of the village for the building of a new school in Fennel Street.

IN 1875, the new Mickleover School Board announced a plan to purchase land "for the erection of New Schools". The piece of land "containing half an acre in a field situate at Mickleover … called Hall Croft now in the occupation of Mr William Bailey, and which said piece of land is bounded on the South by the Turnpike-road, leading from Mickleover to Uttoxeter, on the West by land now of late belonging to Mrs Goodwin and Mr Samuel Wade the younger, on the East by the road leading from Mickleover to Radbourne, and on the North partly by land belonging to Mr Samuel Wade the elder and partly belonging to C. E. Newton Esq"

IN 1881, the new school on Uttoxeter Road opened for older children. In 1905 it was enlarged and, in 1916, the infants, who had remained at Fennel Street, were transferred to the main building.

~~~~~~

IN September 1896, some 250 children attending the mixed and infants' departments of the Mickleover Board School were taken to Manor Park – the grounds of Mickleover Manor – for a special treat. They had been invited by the Newtons and were greeted, on the lawn, by Mrs Newton. The *Derby Daily Telegraph* noted: "Football and other games were feely indulged in till four o'clock when ample justice was done to a most substantial tea." Their teachers were then given an "excellent knife and fork tea". More games followed and at six o'clock Mr Newton bid them farewell. The Newtons were given resounding cheers of appreciation by all their guests. Each child left with a "text card, packet of sweets, and a bun, and the happy party wended its way homewards highly delighted with the day's proceedings".

~~~~~~

ON 7 February 1900, the Infant School Room in Mickleover (now the Community Centre) was the venue for a "one night only" demonstration of the new Bioscope – a very early version of cinema. At 8pm the main show began with "100 Images –

The village schoolroom on Uttoxeter Road was opened in 1881. It now serves as Mickleover Community Centre.

Tour Around the World". Prior to this there was a special show for local children – thus Mickleover was the site of the first children's cinema matinee performance in Britain.

IN the 1950s, the former College for the Training of School Mistresses that stood on Uttoxeter Road in Derby was relocated to Mickleover. The renamed Bishop Lonsdale Teacher Training College was eventually absorbed by Derby College of Further Education and later formed part of the University of Derby.

The laying of the foundation stone at the Bishop Lonsdale Teacher Training College, off Chevin Avenue, in the 1950s.

The site was cleared in recent years and the Varsity Grange housing estate built on its land. The Lonsdale Swimming Pool, once part of the college, remains in situ and is open to the public and used by a variety of local swimming groups.

WHEN Mickleover Manor ceased to be a private residence, it became a private preparatory school for boys aged 5 to 14. The school had its own open-air swimming pool but closed in 1950. The local health authority then took possession and, until 1989 the Manor was used as a home for the elderly.

10
Inns and Taverns

MICKLEOVER has always been well served by its inns and taverns. The Masons' Arms in Etwall Road dates from at least the 18th century, although it has been substantially altered, most notably on its street front, over the years.

The Masons' Arms stands beside what was once the village market square.

Situated beside what was the market square and opposite both the parish church and the manor house, this was likely always the main village pub. The 'masons' in question are believed to be the freemasons. The pub was often the venue for political meetings, and social gatherings.

THE Nag's Head – in name at least – is one of the oldest inns in the village, although the present building, and location, dates only from 1928. The original premises stood at the edge of

The original Nag's Head was part of a range of old buildings that stood between The Square and Limes Avenue. The Masons' Arms can be seen in the distance.

the market square, on the site of what was to become a filling station. In 1848 the *Derby Mercury* featured an advertisement for the sale of the pub, calling it "an old-established public-house".

What was perhaps surprising was that the lot for sale also included "the Butcher's Shop, Brewhouse, Stable, Yard and Garden" as well as "Four Dwelling-houses adjoining". On several occasions boxing matches were held at the pub.

ON the other side of the road, and of much more traditional appearance, The Vine is a very old building indeed and has a timber-framed interior. At one time it had a "living" inn sign with a huge vine growing across the front of the pub. Recently

Over the years The Vine has undergone a number of cosmetic changes, most notably to its chimneys and brickwork.

new grape vines have been planted within the garden of the pub.

A NUMBER of other inns, pubs and beerhouses are mentioned in historical documents. Most often mentioned is the Plough Inn, at Huffin Heath "on the border of Mickleover and Littleover." Situated somewhere between the farms of Huffin Heath and Rough Heanor, it was primarily a beerhouse and would have been a popular stop along the road between Derby and Mickleover itself. The precise site for this pub has never been firmly established. Various locations have been suggested, from the corner of what is now Arundel Avenue to the site of the old Huffin Heath retirement home. Given the evidence of censuses, newspaper reports and maps, it seems more likely that The Plough stood on the south side of Uttoxeter Road and that it was probably located at, or near to, the foot of Chain Lane.

In 1839 the *Derby Mercury* featured an advertisement for the sale of the inn: "All that Old Established and eligibly situated

PUBLIC HOUSE at Huffenheath in the Parish of Mickleover, adjoining the Uttoxeter Turnpike Road distant about 2 miles from Derby, and known by the sign of The Plough, comprising house-place, 2 parlours, bar, brewhouse, cellar, large dining room, 3 lodging rooms, stable, cowhouse, piggery, yard &c. Also a GARDEN and CROFT of excellent meadow land adjoining the same."

In August 1874, former publican James Young reapplied for his license to serve alcohol. However, this was refused on the grounds that he had been repeatedly convicted for breaking the terms of his previous licences.

THE White Hart and the Three Pigeons are mentioned only briefly during the 18th century, it is quite possible that these are alternative names for the Vine. Another beerhouse, The Wheel, is believed to have stood on Etwall Road, on the corner of what is now Orchard Street.

AS the village expanded, additional public houses have been opened. In the early 1880s, an application was made for a new pub to serve the area around the new railway station. The

Mickleover Station has been converted to residential use. It stands alongside the new National Cycle Network Route 68.

case was argued that, with the station more than a mile and a quarter from the centre of the village, there was no pub near the station. As well as a watering hole, decent and comfortable resting facilities were required, especially for farm servants sent to the station to wait collect or deliver goods. Those servants, it was argued, "had to wait there a considerable time without being able to get anything in the shape of refreshment. If the Bench granted a license, they would not be creating a mere drink shop, but they would be conferring a public boon by acceding to the application".

The Great Northern was built to serve passengers arriving at Mickleover Station, as well as labourers delivering there.

Tonman Mosley, representing Benjamin Potter's application, then showed the Bench a petition in favour of the application that was signed by 120 local residents. He added that both the vicars of Mickleover and Radbourne supported the application.

However, some locals were less than keen and their representative argued that "it would be a great temptation to the lads bringing milk to the station".

The Bench had some sympathy to this claim and granted the licence only on the condition that a "large and commodious coffee-room" was added to the already built premises. For a short period, the pub was known as the Northern. It was, of course, today's Great Northern.

11

Fire, Storm and Flood

IN late October 1757, the *Derby Mercury* reported: "One Night last Week a melancholy Accident happen'd at Mickleover Church near this Town where there had been a Fire kept the Day before, which by some unknown means, caught the Seats, and did considerable Damage before it was extinguished. "

IN 1878, the *Edinburgh Evening News*, among other newspapers, reported "A Disgraceful Hoax" at Mickleover. With the village relying on the fire brigade at Burton, it took some time for calls for help to arrive, and a telegram was often used. One Wednesday afternoon such a telegram was sent to Burton police station "informing the authorities that the Mickleover Asylum was in flames".

As the news spread, several families in Burton, who had friends and relatives either working at, or held in the asylum, panicked and began to make their way to Mickleover. "Four fire-engines belonging to the breweries, the town and the county were despatched with the greatest promptitude." But when they, and the worried relatives and friends, arrived in Mickleover, it was clear that there was no fire at all.

ON 12 July 1912, a series of violent thunderstorms swept across Derby. One house on Western Road in Mickleover was struck by lightning. The chimney was demolished and the corner of the house fell down, with part of the roof stripped away and the rafters split. The furniture in one bedroom was blown outside and a considerable amount of other damage was done. Fortunately, there was no one in the house at the time.

Three years later, on 30 June 1915, another great storm passed over the area. This time the downpour seemed concentrated on Mickleover. And it was no ordinary downpour. According to the *Derby Daily Telegraph* it was "a terrific thunderstorm of exceptional violence, accompanied by hailstones ... the lightning was particularly vivid, and the thunder very violent, while the hailstones (large as nuts) fell incessantly for 30 minutes in huge quantities until the ground was covered several inches deep".

It was quite something to behold and "the roadways quickly presented the appearance of rushing torrents, the rain falling in immense volume for over an hour ... Nothing like it has been seen within the memory of anyone at Mickleover ... the hail fell with terrific force, stripping all kinds of vegetation off its foliage and breaking the contents of gardens into pieces ... hundreds of the potato haulms stand bare and broken without a single leaf left on." The path of the worst of the storm was limited to a channel "less than a mile wide, dashing with irresistible force and relentless fury from north to south-east".

ON the evening of Friday, 14 January 1916, Mickleover residents were surprised to experience an earthquake followed by an aftershock.

IN April 1947, residents of Mickleover Hollow had a lucky escape when gales brought down a beech tree on to cottages

The Hollow, looking towards several of Mickleover's listed cottages. Nearest the camera is the Old Hollow Cottage.

The Old Hollow Cottage with its box framing now clearly visible.

there. Fortunately, although there was a great deal of damage caused, the tree fell just after teatime and none of the residents were harmed. One of the four cottages in the row lost its roof. The occupants, Mr and Mrs Brown, told reporters that a little later their small daughter would have been in bed. The roof was never repaired and the cottage remains, to this day, the only single-storey one in the row.

12

Civic Life Could Come to Blows

IN the 19th century local politics certainly aroused passions. Indeed, they could come to blows, as we can see from a report in the *Derby Mercury* in 1885 when John Brook Holmes, a blacksmith, and his son, Thomas, were summoned for assaulting another Mickleover resident, Thomas Riley.

Holmes senior, meanwhile, had brought a cross summons against Riley. The trio had been at a meeting organised by Mr Curzon in the Infant Schoolroom. Mr Riley's representative, told the court that Riley had been one of several people who showed their disapproval of Mr Curzon's views by "hooting in a mild manner". Although Riley had no direct communication with either Holmes, John Holmes had approached him in a "menacing manner" and when Riley moved away, Holmes continued to follow him. When Mr Curzon entered the room, and the hooting commenced, "Holmes struck Riley a violent blow on the side of the face, knocking him to the ground".

As Riley scrambled to his feet, he saw Holmes about to strike another blow and so, using a stick he had taken to the meeting, he struck Holmes on the head, drawing a considerable amount of blood. Young Thomas Holmes went to defend his father and "rushed forward and struck Riley a tremendous blow below the belt which rendered him insensible and he was carried home".

But the Holmes' defence offered quite a different interpretation of events. They held that Riley was at the meeting only to voice his disagreement as one of a group of radicals, that he taken a stick into the meeting with the intention of causing trouble, and had struck Holmes with his stick before any blows had been landed in the other direction and that the younger Holmes had struck no blows at all.

So disparate were the two accounts, with each party able to call corroborating witnesses, that it was clear, in the words of Riley's legal representative "gross perjury had been committed by one side or the other".

Unfortunately, it remained unclear which side this was, and the Bench dismissed all the summonses and ordered each party to pay their own costs.

IN March 1892, the *Derby Daily Telegraph* carried a story headlined: "Mickleover – A Droll Electioneering Incident."

It went on: "When Mr Broad and party made a flying visit to this lackadaisical village the other day, they called upon a most distinguished and eminent personage in the village, well known for his sturdy independence, with the motive of obtaining his vote. After an introduction to the candidate, who asked for his vote, this gentleman, in a off-hand and effervescent kind of way, said: 'I dunner want owt to don wi' onny o' yo chaps; ye no good aonny o' yo, yo mack fine promises to get to Parliament, but when yo get there yo dou nowt; if I'd ony a bit of bread and butter yo'd tak the butter and leave nowt but th' bread for mai'. After the little fiery episode had cooled down, and failing to attain the object much desired, the party went laughing away, evidently much amused, if not disappointed; for with all their electioneering suavity, the firmness of our friend was impregnable. He remained neutral as regards voting for either party."

~~~~~~~~~~~~~~~~~~~~~~

IN January 1932, at the annual general meeting of Mickleover and District Ratepayers' Association, held at the Nag's Head Hotel, appeals from locals for an increase in local policing were on the verge of being turned down due to "the present financial crisis". The same fate was to befall pleas for a footpath along Chain Lane.

Other local concerns were the "sewage nuisance" that "existed on the main road opposite the golf club house" and the committee decided that the County Council and Shardlow Rural Council were to be asked to deal with "the unhealthy and offensive overflow of sewage into Uttoxeter Road".

~~~~~~~~~~~~~~~~~~~~~~

THE Mickleover and District Ratepayers' Association was key in the development of the village. In 1936, they asked the Parish Council to negotiate with Derby Borough Council to allow the village to use the services of the Borough Fire Brigade. There was great local concern that the village, as part of Repton Rural Council, relied upon fire engines dispatched from Burton, which could take as long as 25 minutes to arrive on the scene. It was reckoned that Mickleover could secure the services of the town brigade. Not only would this prove more efficient – arriving in Mickleover within five minutes – it would prove a good economic decision. The extra cost required would amount to as little as 3s 4d per household per year.

~~~~~~~~~~~~~~~~~~~~~~

ONE of the more contentious issues surrounding Mickleover was its very nature. A reader's letter in the *Derby Evening Telegraph* of 18 March 1939 took exception to an article in an earlier issue that described Mickleover and Allestree, as "suburbs" of Derby.

Written by an anonymous "Mickleover Resident", the letter stated: "I cannot help feeling that nobody with any knowledge of Mickleover could have made such a statement.

"Mickleover is joined on to Derby only by ribbon development along Western Road … it is separated from it by two miles of agricultural land, and is three miles distant from the centre of the town."

In the 1940s complaints were aired about the uneven condition of the pavement of Western Road.

The correspondent noted that, aside from newer houses on Western and Station Road, Havenbaulk Lane "and a short avenue or two", that it "consists of a pleasant country village, surrounded on three sides by unspoiled well-farmed land, and enjoys its Women's Institute and its County Library and other rustic pleasures."

"Were it to come into the borough it would forfeit both these advantages for the doubtful privilege of having its dust collected more competently and of trolley-buses with their urbanising influence and unsightly poles and wires."

So outraged was the writer, at the prospect of Mickleover being absorbed into the Borough, that they suggested Derby "turn its attention to Littleover – a suburb … in the real sense of the word."

IN October 1935, the *Derby Evening Telegraph* reported: "Derby Aerodrome Site Decision Opposed At Mickleover"

With the growth of air travel, Derby Corporation felt it essential that the town establish an aerodrome within easy reach of the population. They identified a piece of land straddling Mackworth, Radbourne and Mickleover as topographically the most suitable. In Mickleover this was received with little enthusiasm.

Living in a village that had been developed as a purely residential area, people there drew up a resolution that they intended to send to the Air Ministry, objecting to the plans. They argued that the noise associated with the project would be harmful to patients at the County and Borough mental hospitals, as well as at the City Hospital and Boundary House (the new name for the old workhouse). Many also feared a drop in the value of their properties, although Mr F. S. Cowlishaw, secretary of Mickleover Ratepayers' Association, argued: "Looking ahead and taking the long view, the presence of an aerodrome might tend to enhance property in the immediate neighbourhood." However, the Borough Council was persuaded. The following year it moved its plans to a site at nearby Burnaston. Whilst Etwall residents now began to plan their own protest, Mickleover folk breathed a sigh of relief.

IN January 1949 Mr S. A. Clarke attended a meeting of Mickleover Parish Council to ask that something be done about the "bad condition" of the pavements in the parish. Mr Clarke claimed: "In Western Road there were large holes which were constantly filled with water. In frosty weather the water froze and was a grave danger to the public."

In July a menace of another kind was causing concern. Residents of Jackson Avenue were suffered a plague of ants "which have invaded gardens and houses, seething masses of them hiding in every nook and cranny".

The *Derby Evening Telegraph* reported that when one resident disturbed a column of winged ants on her lawn, "some of them flew in her hair", while a flock of greedy birds snapped up the rest. Residents had tried everything to deter them, from disinfectant to paraffin and even by setting fire to the ground where they crawled. They appealed to readers to provide some solution.

~~~~~~

IN 1950, "A Mickleover Rate-payer for 23 years" wrote to the *Derby Evening Telegraph* in a confused state regarding the rules and regulations of the dustbin collection: "I have given all clean newspapers to the fishmonger, used greasy ones to light the fire, burnt what food I could, mixed potato peelings with slack, put vegetable matter on the compost heap, and when the dustman emptied the dustbin this morning he stood at the gate, took out a little red notebook and pencil and made a note of my address. I admit I did put ashes, milk bottle tops, a broken plate and food I could not burn (wrapped well up in newspaper) in the dustbin. Have I done wrongly?"

~~~~~~

13

Law and Disorder

PERHAPS unsurprisingly, a point of great concern to Mickleover residents has always been that of law and order. It is easy to imagine that the village has always been a quiet, largely trouble-free place to live. However, seemingly modern problems like anti-social behavior are nothing new. Throughout the years complaints of arrests for drunkenness, of problems between neighbours and of general disturbances in Mickleover have featured at numerous court hearings. Indeed, modern Mickleover residents almost certainly enjoy a more peaceful existence than most of their predecessors.

Indeed, in the 1790s, so concerned were Mickleover folk about the threat of crime that they formed the "Mickleover Association for Prosecuting Felons, etc".

Punishments, particularly in the 18th and 19th century, were draconian and seldom was any convicted criminal treated with understanding or sensitivity.

On 6 December 1786, Thomas Taylor and William Soar were tried at Derby for stealing "a Quantity of Lead from Bareward Coat near Mickleover" Taylor, it seemed, already had a criminal record, having been tried six years earlier for "breaking open a Shop at Alvaston". He had received the death sentence for that conviction, but had been reprieved and instead had been "sent to the Thames" – in other words, to one of the prison hulks moored on the river in London. The writer of the report in the *Derby Mercury* could not hold back their sarcasm, noting that he had made the most of his time in gaol, adding "from which Academy he was discharged, after staying his allotted Time, and where, there is no Doubt, he completed his Education". Both men were sent to the County Gaol.

WHAT we would now regard as muggings were disturbingly common. In 1787 Joseph Pegge was charged with "assaulting Robert Stone in the Foot-road from Mickleover to Burnaston, and taking from him one Shilling in Silver, a Canvas Bag containing a Guinea and a Half in Gold, and his Watch". Fortunately for Pegge, the evidence was vague enough that he was acquitted. Others attending the same Assizes were not so lucky, with sentences of whipping, imprisonment and even death handed out that day.

IN December 1884, Walter Wagg, a boiler maker, and Alfred Walker, a labourer, both of Littleover were charged with violently assaulting John Perceval, a Derby clog dancer, as he made his way back from Mickleover wakes. He told police that, just before he reached Chain Lane, the two men "seized him and took money (2s) from his coat pocket. However, several weeks later the court heard that the police were now unable to find Perceval, who had failed to appear on two previous occasions. The prisoners' representative argued that the story was uncorroborated "and it was probable that, feeling that he could not support the charge, he had bolted". Since the case could not be proved without the participation of Perceval and since both youths had previously good characters, they were discharged.

IN 1870, John Brassington, landlord of the Masons' Arms, appeared in court charged with assaulting Henry Dean, a retired businessman, and "stealing from him two pocket-books, a cheque for £600, a purse containing a sovereign, two half-sovereigns and 18s in silver". The crime took place "on the high road at Mickleover".

Dean had been on his way to his home in Burnaston from a meeting in Derby. He went into the Masons' Arms for a drink. He had been "a little in liquor" when he had arrived and "became more fresh" whilst there. But, apparently, "not too much in liquor to give a good account of what he had in his possession when he entered the house" and "not so drunk that he could not walk." He remembered there being some conversation about a pigeon shooting match. Someone asked him if he would like to join in and he declined. He also claimed that he had declined the offer of a drink, and the glass of gin that was offered to him. When Dean left the pub, the landlord followed.

"I do not know what passed after until getting on to the road leading to the asylum. I then saw a man standing by the roadside. Immediately after another person came to me, pushed me down and took my money and the pocket books. The men then ran away."

Dean returned immediately to the pub. There he found Brassington who did not seem surprised when Dean told him he had been robbed, remarking only: "Have you?" Dean then went back out to find a policeman to whom he could report the crime.

Suspicion fell quite quickly on Brassington and he, and another man, a regular of the pub, John Webster, who also went by the name of John Buxton, were arrested. Webster told the court that the landlord had taken him to one side and told him that he had "seen some money in Dean's possession". Brassington then suggested: "Let us go and take the bugger's money."

Webster stated that he had cautioned against his. Then Brassington suggested giving the visitor some gin to make him drunk before taking his money. Eventually, Webster did go with Brassington, although the pair left by different exits and arranged to meet up on Asylum Lane. This they did with Brassington apparently telling Webster: "As you are very fresh, I'll do the job". After the deed was done the pair hurried back to the Masons' Arms by different routes.

The following day Webster returned to the pub and was told by Brassington that he had also stolen a cheque for £600. Webster could not read so had no way of confirming whether or not this was true, but he advised the innkeeper to get rid of the cheque. Some time later Webster saw Brassington and he confirmed that he had disposed of the cheque.

In court, however, Brassington told a different story. He claimed that while at the Masons' Arms, Dean had become progressively drunk. That he had shown his money to all those present. That he had only accompanied Dean to the top of the steps and then had bid him goodnight. That Dean had returned a short time later and announced that he had been robbed.

When first questioned about the incident, Brassington had suggested to the police that they make enquiries of a woman with whom Dean had spent most of the afternoon. However, a number of witnesses had seen Brassington, Webster and Dean at various places along the route towards the location of the robbery.

By the time of the trial, that December, a new publican by the name of Frederick Gregory was running the Masons' Arms. Gregory gave evidence to the court. Some time after he had taken over he "received some information about a receipt" (a cheque) and had found a banker's receipt wrapped up and placed in a "little nick in the ceiling" of the pub's garret. The jury deliberated for only a few minutes and found Brassington guilty.

Causing a great sensation, the judge passed a sentence of 10 years' penal servitude. The case made the headlines right across the country, the *Paisley and Renfrewshire Advertiser* colourfully calling it a "Daring Highway Robbery by an Innkeeper".

SOME people came into contact with the authorities more than others. William Hodgkinson of Huffin Heath Farm was one such man, sometimes as a perpetrator, others as a victim. In June 1845, he was "committed to hard labour for six weeks" for an assault upon George and Charlotte Dakin, although no explanation to the nature of the assault, or the events that had led to it were reported.

In 1857, Henry Moore of Ashbourne Road in Derby took Hodgkinson to court to "recover from defendant the sum of £36 10s 4d for the balance of account in respect of the building of two cottages." After the plaintiff's lawyer had outlined the case, the judge made it quite clear that he thought it was "a very improper case to be submitted to a jury and suggested that it should be left to a competent builder". It seemed that there was more to the dispute than might at first appear. Hodgkinson's representative, Mr Borough, "thought that if a reference took place it should be of all matters in dispute between the parties, and he could not consent to it in any other way".

Moore had agreed to build for Hodgkinson two cottages for £150. This had been paid, without delay, but Moore now wished to be paid for "extras". There was a short debate while either party engaged witnesses to prove, or disprove, the value of these extras. The jury found in favour of the plaintiff and determined that Hodgkinson pay, not only the outstanding money, but Moore's legal costs too.

But Hodkingson was not in court to learn his fate. His lawyer had told the court that he was "sorry the defendant was so intoxicated that he was afraid he could not call him".

In 1860, Hodgkinson purchased some meat from a butcher in Sadler Gate, which he told the butcher he would collect later. At some point after leaving the butcher, Hodgkinson must have spoken about his purchase either to a man named James Poyser, or within his earshot, because later that afternoon Poyser arrived at the butcher's and told them he had been sent to collect the meat. He took a piece, weighing about 18lbs, to the Elephant and Castle on Bold Lane where he exchanged it for some drink. Poyser pleaded guilty and was sentenced to "six calendar months' imprisonment with hard labour".

Five years later, just after Christmas, the *Derby Mercury* reported " a dirty young fellow, who gave the name of Albert Else was charged with stealing £21 in gold from the person of William Hodkinson (sic), farmer, of Huffin Heath". Hodgkinson had been in the Rowditch Inn. "In celebration of the festive season," he had treated Else and several others to drinks. Else "knowing that the prosecutor had a bag of gold, frolicked with him, and in the confusion the gold and the bag were lost".

According to the newspaper, Hodgkinson amused the court with his banter, telling the Mayor, who was on the Bench "This is the first time I have had the pleasure of appearing before you and I hope it will be the last!"

The Mayor: "Your case is remanded till this day week"

Hodgkinson: "And quite right too. I'll give him bellows to mend. I was treating them all round and they robbed all the time."

However, when the case came back to court, the policeman in charge told the Bench that Hodgkinson was "in an unfit state to appear before you". The officer conceded that, "although there is no doubt of the robbery we cannot, in the absence of the prosecutor and the witnesses, ask you for a further remand".

Else's solicitor then told the court that he had proof that the man was not involved in the robbery. With no evidence being offered against him, Else was discharged and Hodgkinson's robber remained at large.

~~~~~~

IN January 1865, George Bantam was "summoned for being drunk and riotous at Mickleover". He had left the Nag's Head

The Nag's Head opened in its current location in 1928.

on Boxing Day in a "very drunk" state and when asked to go home "swore and used very bad language". He was fined 5s and costs.

~~~~~~

WITH the arrival of the Great Northern Railway came dozens of workers to Mickleover. Many of them were navies and there were a number of unpleasant incidents involving them. One of the most unpleasant occurred in 1876 and resulted in Thomas Chambers being sentenced to six months' hard labour. He had been found guilty of the attempted assault of 75-year-old Mary Porter. Mrs Porter's husband went to milk the cows. Chambers entered the house, locked the door and "attempted to criminally assault the old lady, whom he treated shamefully". Fortunately Mr Porter returned to the house and "interrupted him in his villainy". Chambers escaped through an upstairs window, but was arrested a short time later.

Fortunately, most of the crime connected with the navvies was less disturbing in nature, but it was certainly extensive. In

August 1877, the *Derby Mercury* reported that much of the Derby County Bench's day had been taken up in hearing cases against navvies employed on the Great Northern Railway at Mickleover. It seemed that several had been making a good profit, without paying taxes, by selling beer and spirits to their workmates. Two undercover police officers had obtained work on the railway and were lodging with one of the navvies. The policemen had made themselves at home and asked whether there was a public house nearby, where he could get ale and food. The landlady told them that she could supply it and went into her bedroom and brought out a quart of ale, for which the policemen paid 6d. Later that day they asked whether they could have another quart and, again, it was sold for 6d. That evening one of the officers saw several men arrive and leave having purchased ale. The next day one officer bought a quart at breakfast, one at dinner and another at night. He made a record of these sales in a book that he hid "under the hedge".

Both policemen were present when uniformed officers raided the premises where they found an 18-gallon cask, half full of beer and "several jugs" about. The house of another navvy was entered "on consequence of hearing music" where police found "upwards of a score of persons ... some of them being drunk". Here, too, the policemen were sold beer. The police told the court that the same thing had happened at the huts of other navvies. A local horse-keeper, Thomas Bentley, also stood accused. One of the policemen testified that he had watched a drunken man enter Mr Bentley's cottage. They followed him inside. Bentley's wife, it seemed, had her suspicions about the two men, asking them if they were policemen, then deciding they were soldiers. The pair told her they were with "the Rifles". Throwing caution aside she, too, sold them beer.

A similar situation had been found at the house of John Edwards. This time, thinking "they had had sufficient" they asked for only a pint. Mrs Edwards served them without question. When the police raided the properties they found gallons of beer, various bottles of beer and larger bottles of spirits. All the defendants were found guilty and each fined £10 with costs and the penalty of one month's imprisonment with hard labour. They were all cautioned by the Bench and were told that what they had done "injured the legitimate trader" and that, if they should be caught again, the fine would be ten times higher. The seized ale and spirits was to be sold by auction.

IN July 1880, "two respectable boys" – Frederick Norton and Thomas Merry - were charged by Thomas Riley of Mickleover with "trampling over his mowing grass, and doing damage to the extent of 1 shilling". Local police constable Etherington said that one afternoon, while he was walking on the turnpike road, he saw the defendants in a field of mowing grass. Mr Riley said he "wished the Bench to be lenient, but this trespassing had become an intolerable nuisance". Norton was fined 1s and 9s 9d costs, but Merry, who had initially given the policeman a false name, was fined 5s.

IN 1828, Edward Jinkins and Thomas Barns were sent for trial at Chesterfield for "stealing a goose at Mickleover, the property of Philip Radford".

IN August 1881 a "tramp", Robert Ashton, was charged with stealing beans from a field at Mickleover, the property of Mr Riley. He was remanded in custody.

IN 1883, Mickleover played its little part in a dramatic tragedy that grabbed newspaper headlines across the country. Emmanuel Jackson, a noted balloonist, shot his wife "with a six-chambered revolver" at his Burton Road home in Derby.

Then he shot himself. The couple's daughter, who lived with her parents, found the bodies. Remarkably, just days earlier, Jackson had taken an aerial fight in his balloon "Evening Star" from the Arboretum. A sudden heavy thunderstorm had caused him to make an emergency landing at Rough Heanor on the edge of Mickleover, to the great excitement of locals. Jackson, however, declared at the time that it would be the last balloon flight he would make, although no-one could have anticipated the action he was about to take.

～～～～～～～～～～～～～～～～～～～～～～～～

IN February 1884 the *Derby Mercury* reported a gruesome and very sad case under the headline "Discovery of Human Remains At Mickleover".

The remains were identified as those of a newborn child "very unscientifically cut up" and were found close to the Mickleover Asylum. Initially only a child's hand had been found. Thomas Bailey, who was attending to an asylum sewage outlet in a field belonging to Mr Ayre, found the tiny hand in a stream in the middle of the field. Although police made a search, nothing further was found until two days later when another labourer found a child's foot in the same stream. The sewage tank, which emptied into the field, was then searched and four more discoveries were made – a right thigh, left shoulder blade and arm, left forearm and part of the ribs and back. The gender was unclear, and it could not be ascertained whether the baby had been born alive, but it was clear that the remains had been there "some three or four weeks, perhaps longer".

It seemed likely that the body parts could only have reached the sewage tank via the drains, which had been reported to be blocked slightly on several days around Christmas time. Dr James Murray Lindsay, the superintendent physician at the Asylum, testified that, to his knowledge, no pregnant patient had been resident at the Asylum during the previous six months and that they had not had on the premises the body of any child for dissection or the like. Several weeks of investigation yielded no further clues and an inquest jury recorded "that the deceased's remains were found in a field and sewage tank, but how or by what means they were placed there, there was no evidence to show".

IN June 1886, Henry Davis "was charged with uttering a forged cheque for £6 5s with intent to cheat and defraud Mr C. E. Newton of Mickleover Manor". Davis had been working at the Manor as a footman. He had "cashed a cheque with Mary Rattican, wife of Thomas Rattican, of the Nag's Head, which turned out to be a forgery." But by the time a warrant was issued for his arrest, Davis had already fled and set sail for America. Several months later, in November, he had returned to England and enlisted with the 6th Dragoon Guards. When he arrived at Canterbury, he was arrested on a warrant. At a later hearing Davis pleaded guilty. He was sentenced to six months' hard labour.

IN 1893, the home of the Sugitt family in The Hollow was the scene of an alleged attempted murder. Police were called to the house and found Fanny Bates, a resident of Derby and the wife of Midland Railway coach painter Edward Bates, "in a helpless and prostrate condition ... She had lost a very large quantity of blood from a deep wound in the neck and several severe cuts on the face." A doctor had been called and Mrs Bates' wounds had been dressed.

It seemed that, in a jealous rage, her husband had attacked her. When he appeared at the Assizes, it took the jury only 20 minutes to find Edward Bates guilty of causing grievous bodily harm. He was sent to prison for 18 months "with hard labour".

14

"Outrage At Mickleover Manor – Discovery of a Bomb"

I
N 1893, Mickleover was the scene of a dramatic story that was reported in newspapers across the country. The *Nottingham Evening Post* described it: "Supposed Attempted Outrage At Mickleover Manor – Discovery of a Bomb."

The newspaper continued: "An extraordinary and startling discovery is reported from Mickleover Manor, the residence of Mr C. E. Newton JP. A few mornings ago Miss Margaret Newton, who happened to be the only member of the family at home, found a tin canister on the windowsill of the library. It had a long fuse attached, and this was partially burnt. On further examining the tin it was found to contain about half a pound of gunpowder, which had it exploded, would undoubtedly have shattered the large plate glass window of the library, and done considerable damage to various articles in the vicinity." It had been a lucky escape, with the fuse burning "to within an inch or two of the gunpowder".

The old Mickleover Manor today. All Saints' Church is visible in the distance.

Only the damp condition of the windowsill had extinguished it.

The *Lincolnshire Echo* expanded upon the report stating that Mr Newton had "lately received a threatening letter" and that Miss Newton had found the "shell" on the outside windowsill of the dining room and, upon investigation had found another such device under the window.

A suspect was soon identified. Within days, William Blood, a local labourer, was arrested and remanded into custody. Unexpectedly, a few hours later Blood was released on bail on his own recognisance. He had vehemently protested his innocence and, it seemed, the police suspected the young man might be telling the truth. As the *Derby Daily Telegraph* reported: "Blood's innocence is not yet proved, but in view of the doubt which exists in regard to him, Supt Daybell very properly took immediate steps to release the prisoner from custody."

Another man, Samuel Staton, a labourer at the County Asylum, was subsequently arrested. Described as "little more than a boy" he faced four charges. That he "feloniously placed a canister of gunpowder on the windowsill of the Manor House with intent to kill or injure divers persons there on 15 May, that he did unlawfully and maliciously send on 13 April a certain letter to Mr C. E. Newton JP, threatening to kill and murder, and further, with sending similar letters to Miss Margaret Newton on 6 May, and to Mr John Hodson on 28 December 1893."

By the time the *Derby Daily Telegraph* of 1 June 1894 reported on the "Magisterial Inquiry" into an event it now called "The Mickleover Sensation", the investigation had moved on apace.

The Newtons, it seemed, had been receiving a number of threatening letters "for some time past" and that, in consequence of these, the head gardener, Mr Campbell, had been instructed, in future, to open all letters "in the handwriting in question and to hand them over to the police".

One letter sent to Miss Newton was read out in court:

"Miss – your father having refused me money, I shall now proceed to take my revenge. I came on Monday night and placed the can of powder against your window. That is but a sample of what is going to follow, as I shall use dynamite in large quantities which will shake the Manor to its foundations. I will give you one word of advise (*sic*), get another dog as the one you have now passed within a few feet of me and could not see me. It is of no use calling in the police, as I defy them. I saw the Mickleover sergeant and Supt Daybell at the Manor on Thursday and I shall put a bullet into both of them if they give me any more nonsense. They are useless in this case. My blow will fall when it is least expected, leaving death and destruction behind. You will greatly oblige by showing this letter to the sergeant and Supt Daybell. You cannot escape my vengeance in going to Jaffa, as your father had done."

The letter was signed "Jay Hawk"

A short postscript warned: "A false friend is more to be feared than an open foe; show this letter to those thief-catchers. Catch me if you can. Beware – J. H."

Mickleover's Postmistress proved a vital witness in the case of the "Mickleover Bomb". An incriminating letter was posted here.

The postmistress remembered precisely the time this letter had been posted, since she had just cleared the box when it dropped down. She had read the address "Miss Margaret Newton, Esquire" (which had provided much amusement in court) and placed it with the other post.

Two witnesses had seen Staton posting a letter at the Post Office, at the time that the offending letter had been sent. He was also known to be in possession of a six-chamber revolver that he had shown to a companion and to his own brother. However, when the police conducted a search, the revolver could not be found.

The court heard that a sample of Staton's handwriting had been taken and compared, by an expert, to that in the letters. "There was a strong similarity," was the expert opinion.

Perhaps even more damning was the evidence given by William Briggs, a friend of Staton, who testified that Staton had shown him the revolver and had told him that the Newtons had received some letters "which had swearing in and wanting money, and that they had gone to Jaffa out of the way because they were afraid".

Staton's 14-year-old brother told the magistrates that his brother told him he had bought "a life preserver" and showed him the revolver which he said he had bought from Harry Wall, a former employee of Mr Newton, for about 2s 6d.

As for the "bomb", there was other evidence to consider. The canister, it seemed, was "an ordinary large size sardine box". When the police arrived, Miss Newton had had one of the servants place it in a bucket of water.

Mr Rosson, a gunmaker, testified that it contained ordinary sporting gunpowder, and had a homemade fuse – "an ordinary piece of string saturated with salt petre and nitre." However, it was his opinion that, had it exploded, considerable damage would have been done. Not only would the window have been blown out but "if any persons had been in the room they would probably have been severely injured".

Other letters, allegedly written by Staton, were read out in court, including one telling Mr Hodson that "a gentleman living at Mickleover" demanded "a purse of money" be concealed outside his drive and threatening to take "revenge out of your daughters as well" if this was not done. "You need not be at all surprised if one of them turns up missing." Again the handwriting was likened to that of Staton.

In July 1894, Samuel Staton pleaded guilty to the charges. In his defence, he stated that his had "been in the habit of reading "penny dreadfuls".

As the *Derby Mercury* summarized: "The police discovered that it was the mad freak of a lad in the village whose mind had evidently been disordered by the reading of cheap trashy novels."

Young Staton "expressed contrition and promised reformation". He was sentenced to one month's hard labour.

15

Tragic Deaths, Mysterious Disappearances

ON 14 February 1753 the *Derby Mercury* reported: "Yesterday Morning Mr Abraham Hurst of Mickleover, late a Dyer at Darley near this Town, was found accidentally drown'd in a little Brook betwixt Littleover and Mickleover. He had been [on] a small Journey the Day before, and was on his Return Home. As his Horse was not far from him, and the Saddle, with the Mail Pillion, and some Goods, were found about a Quarter of a Mile from the Place where he was drown'd, 'tis supposed, (the Girth being broke) that he was thrown from his Horse, who going forwards, in order to get before and catch him, he went through some Closes and going over a small Wooden Bridge or Plank, leading into the Lane again, 'tis thought his Feet flipp'd, and being entangled, could not disengage himself."

WITH open fireplaces and other dangers, life in the late 18th century could be perilous. On Christmas Day 1771, Alice

Bailey suffered fatal burns. According to the report in the *Derby Mercury*: "It was supposed she was taken with a Fit (in the Absence of her husband, who had left her but a few Minutes before) and falling into the Fire, was burnt in a shocking Manner, her Face etc being a perfect Cynder when she was found."

In 1804, young Hannah Ratcliffe, a six-year-old Mickleover girl, suffered a similar fate. According to the *Derby Mercury*: "Her mother imprudently left it alone whilst she went to the Bakehouse, and on her return found it in flames.

IN 1895, the authorities were investigating the death of David Willis, a 49-year-old widowed platelayer who had been sent out in sub-zero temperatures, and in a heavy snowstorm, on a January afternoon to make an inspection of the railway line at Mickleover. While he was inside the Mickleover tunnel and "screened from observation" one passenger train and a light engine entered the tunnel from opposite directions. Not long afterwards his body "run over and mangled", and with severe head injuries, was found by a ganger. His body was removed to Mickleover Station until after the coroner's inquiry that was held at the neighbouring Great Northern Hotel.

TIMES were hard for many and some were tempted to take desperate measures. In March 1880, the *Derby Telegraph* reported that the "well-known Derbyshire farmer, Mr William Calladine of the Rough Heanor Farm, committed suicide on Tuesday under very painful circumstances. He got up between six and seven in the morning and left the house without taking breakfast. As he did not return within a reasonable time, a search was made, but his body was not found until evening. The deceased was discovered in a ditch, with a tremendous wound in his throat, evidently inflicted with a razor, which he

Rough Heanor Farm, on the eastern edge of the parish.

had in his hand. The deceased was only married a second time a few weeks ago. It is said he had of late been troubled about business matters."

IN 1888, Matthew Clark, landlord of the Vine Inn, committed suicide by hanging himself in a cowshed. "He was quite dead."

OCCASIONALLY a criminal act was committed and in the most desperate of circumstances. In February 1883, an inquest was held at Radbourne Common Farm into the death of an unnamed male child who had been born three days earlier. He was the child of 20-year-old domestic servant, Sarah Jane Swann. It seemed Miss Swann had complained of feeling unwell and retired. She had been seen by her employer, Mary Smith, making several visits to the outside closet. She was "looking very unwell". Mrs Smith eventually insisted that Miss Swann open the door where she found a very disturbing scene. The servant and her clothing were bloodstained. Mrs Smith took the girl back into the house where she "gave her some tea and brandy and water". The girl "fainted away, but soon came around ... "

Mrs Smith put her to bed and brought her some gruel.

She then returned to the closet with a neighbour, Mrs Allcock, and they found the body of a child in the cesspool.

Dr Copestake, who was called to the scene that afternoon, noted that the baby's throat had been cut "to the spine". The newspaper report featured a rather graphic and detailed description of the post mortem after which Dr Copestake and another physician were both of the opinion that the child had probably been born alive, but that there was insufficient evidence to know this for certain.

While the young and unmarried girl had done everything possible to conceal her condition, it had proved fruitless since Mrs Smith stated that she had repeatedly asked whether she might be pregnant or, in the delicate parlance of the day "enceinte". Miss Swann denied this.

Mrs Allcock, told the court that she, too, had asked Miss Swann the same question and had received the same denial. She also stated that, upon the discovery of the baby's tiny body, that Miss Swann had admitted that she was the mother. When asked why she had done what she had done, Miss Swann had replied: "I think the devil had got hold of me."

After a trial the following April, and under the guidance of the judge, who recommended that they "ought not to press the case too tightly against her", the jury found Miss Swann guilty, not of "having feloniously, wilfully, and of malice aforethought, killed and murdered her newly-born male child", but of "concealment of birth".

The judge then ruled that, since she had "been in custody for some time, and that at the time the offence was committed she must have been in great mental and bodily agony", she should serve a sentence of four months.

SOME deaths were simply mysterious. The *Derby Mercury* of 4 December 1889 reported on an inquest of an unknown man whose body had been found on a Mickleover farm several days earlier. It had been found, by labourer Joseph Harlow, underneath hay in a barn belonging to farmer Edward Wade on Asylum Lane.

John Hiley, a taskmaster from Derby's Union Workhouse, told the inquest that he believed the man was known to him as someone who had visited the "casual ward" about a month earlier, which coincided with the length of time the deceased was believed to have been in the barn. It seemed that while the man had clearly managed to get into the barn, the amount of hay stored there meant that it would have been much more difficult to get out.

ON Monday 21 March 1932, the main front-page headline on the *Derby Evening Telegraph* was about the bizarre and tragic death of a local man. Lewis Tomlin, a 61-year-old coachbuilder of Uttoxeter Road, had been reported missing two days earlier. An intensive search by police and neighbours had yielded nothing and neither had interviews with his friends in Derby. The search was eventually redoubled to include a small workshop at the back of the Tomlin home. Inside was a chest. When the locked lid was eventually prised open, "the watchers were amazed to find Mr Tomlin lying dead inside." He was in a seated position with his head bent downward.

A number of theories were advanced to explain the shocking discovery. The chest was not very large, measuring only 24 inches long, 19 inches wide and 24 inches deep. One theory suggested that Mr Tomlin, who was described as a "frail man", had collapsed while standing over the chest, fallen in and the lid had dropped shut on him. The chest had an automatic spring lock that could not be opened from the inside. Another theory was that he had been sitting on the edge of the chest when the lid came down and stunned him, causing him to fall into the box.

Sarah Tomlin, the dead man's sister, was questioned at length. She had last seen her brother alive around 4.45pm on the Thursday. Her brother had appeared agitated and muttered: "It is no use, we can't go on indefinitely like this."

Miss Tomlin explained that her brother had been worrying about his inability to work and that he wanted to get back "on the labour again". She said that she "spoke rather sharply to him".

As she went to get tea ready, her brother left the house. Some time later she had gone into the workshop to tell him his tea was ready but could not find him. She stated that before raising the alarm she had initially assumed he had gone to visit one of their brothers.

As the investigation progressed, it transpired that Miss Tomlin had objected to the chest being searched. She told the coroner that this was because her brother kept his private papers in it and that it was always kept locked.

Percival Tomlin, a local blacksmith and the victim's brother, told the court he had asked his sister whether his brother could be in the chest, but that she had said it was "such silliness" and that they should wait until he returned before they opened it. The following day, with his sister absent, Percival and an older brother had broken open the chest, where they found their missing sibling

A neighbour testified that he had heard knocking from Mr Tomlin's workshop, but had assumed the man had been working.

The coroner told the Tomlins that he thought they should have opened the chest earlier and that Percival ought to have insisted this happen, regardless of his sister's reservations.

The coroner concluded it would probably never be discovered just how Mr Tomlin had come to be inside the chest. There was no evidence to prove foul play or violence, or to suggest that he had deliberately climbed inside. He had, it seemed, died from asphyxia. He recorded an open verdict.

~~~~~~

WHILE Mickleover was a largely safe and caring community, youngsters sometimes found life outside the village was anything but. In April 1912 a dramatic and tragic story emerged. The NSPCC, which had been formed less than 30 years earlier, were prosecuting a farmer and his wife for a "Mickleover Girl's Story of Shocking Cruelty".

Elsie Meeson, the 15-year-old daughter of "most respectable parents at Mickleover", had been working as a servant at a farm in Kilburn. She had been in very good health and had taken "plenty of clothing" with her. Five months later she returned home "in anything but a decently clothed and proper condition". It seemed that for the entire five months she had been ill-treated, receiving food only once a day "and then it was scraps that others had left". An old man who worked in the fields at the farm had felt so sorry for her that he had shared his food with her. "She was seldom or never allowed near the fire to warm herself of dry her clothes."

She was often forced to sleep on the floor in the scullery. The mistress of the house slept in the kitchen, as did the manservant, while the master slept upstairs with his three children – "a domestic arrangement calling for some little explanation".

Elsie had once fallen asleep while chopping sticks and had been awoken by the manservant throwing water over her. One of her tasks was to "journey through the fields in all weathers to turn on and off a water tap". Sometimes she had to do this four times a day. The last of these trips generally took place at 11pm and she was allowed no lantern. "Her clothes froze to her in frosty weather" but she "was not allowed to approach the fire until after the family were asleep".

When she caught taking milk because she was hungry, she had been beaten. Her clothes were never properly washed. If she did this herself she was prevented from drying them.

At Christmas time she was told that she ought to make her employers presents and, when she did not, presents – a box of cigarettes, an overall and several boxes of chocolates – were bought anyway and the cost was taken from her wages.

The local postman had noticed her deteriorating condition and had offered to help her, but Elsie was too afraid to accept, or even tell him her home address. When her mother did come to collect her she declared: "God forbid that my child should come to this!" She was taken home and a doctor called. "It was the most horrible spectacle of a human creature he had ever seen," he told the court.

Despite their assertions that Elsie had been well treated, the farmers were each fined £10, with an alternative of two months with hard labour.

Life back in Common End, Mickleover, must have seemed luxurious by comparison.

~~~~~~

IN 1836, the *Derby Mercury* featured a notice requesting help in finding a missing man. Under the heading "Left His Home", it described one Samuel Bailey as "21 years of age, stands about 5 feet 8 or 9 inches, slender made, and dark hair. Had on when he went away a blue smock frock, fustian trowsers, and black straw hat". His father, John Bailey, was so worried that the notice informed the public: "Whoever will bring, or give information of the said Samuel Bailey … shall be handsomely rewarded for their trouble." At that time he had been missing for more than a week.

~~~~~~

IN May 1907 there was great concern in the village when George Radford, the 13-year-old son of Henry Radford of

Common End, and an errand boy for a business in Derby, was reported missing. He had left home when his parents discovered that for the past five weeks he had spent all his wages and yet told them he had not been paid. The *Derby Daily Telegraph* reporter was of the opinion that "neither his father or the wife [George had a stepmother] troubled very much about him for some time because it was not until Saturday last [4 May] that they reported the case to the police". George had run away on 6 April.

A young friend of the missing boy, Richard Brown, told police that he had seen him on Nottingham Road in Derby and that he "had a fondness for association with travelling showmen and such people and his disappearance dates from the end of the Easter fair".

How long young George was missing is unknown but, happily, the 1911 census shows him living with his father and stepmother in Mickleover.

IN 1918 another resident was reported missing. This time it was 35-year-old Henry Ride of Coomb Crest, Western Road. He was described at 5ft 8in tall, slim build, dark hair and eyes, and wearing a grey suit, fawn cap, brown boots, and gold signet ring on left hand. He was riding a Campion cycle with a child's saddle on the bar. He had left his home at 9.45am on a Friday morning to go to a solicitor's office in St Mary's Gate in Derby but had never arrived.

16

"Too small for disposing properly of the slops"

RIGHT up to the mid-20th century, the spread of infectious disease was regularly detailed. In 1884, local newspapers reported that there was an outbreak of typhoid fever – a disease usually spread by unsanitary conditions and a lack of hygiene – in Derby. The outbreak had originated in late August, at what was now a small farm "in the lane between Littleover and Mickleover, which was formerly known as the Old Plough Inn". This was a small beerhouse that stood at the foot of the old part of Chain Lane.

At this time two families, the Loughenburys and the Beardmores, were tenants. In August, a two-and-a-half-year-old child had come down with typhoid fever and had been admitted to the Infirmary. A few days later, other members of her family fell ill with the same sickness and were also hospitalised. Deputy Chief Constable Lawson took out a summons against Mr Loughenbury for "having, whilst in contact with typhoid fever patients, milked the cows and handled the dairy utensils".

An aerial view of Mickleover before the building of the Silverhill Estate.

Milk from the farm was supplied to a dealer in Litchurch. People who had purchased that milk had also come down with typhoid. When Mr Loughenbury himself became ill, Lawson applied to withdraw the summons. By October there had been more than 100 cases attributable to that source. One death had occurred.

The following February there was another outbreak, this time centred on a cottage in Poke Lane, although on this occasion the victim was convinced that he had been exposed to the disease in Derby. There were concerns, however, that it would be difficult to prevent the spread of the disease throughout Mickleover since "the garden was too small for disposing properly of the slops". Letters were written to the Surveyor of Highways at Etwall "asking him to clean out the ditch … and he had suggested that the ditch should be piped and carried under the highway".

17

Mickleover at War 1914-1918

IN August 1914, at the outbreak of what would become known as the Great War, there was huge enthusiasm at the opportunity to serve King and Country. Then the reality of a new kind of war began to sink in. As the bad news from the front began to filter back home, families who had cheerily waved farewell to their loved ones, certain that before long they would be back home, began to understand that they were not likely to be reunited in the short term, if at all.

The village of Mickleover soon began to feel the effects, when the first refugees from countries invaded by Germany began to arrive in Britain. In October 1914, the *Derby Evening Telegraph* reported: "Two families of Belgian refugees unexpectedly arrived at Derby last evening, and though there was no one to meet them ... the Midland Railway Company's officials proved equal to the occasion."

The refugees, who brought with them nothing save "little bundles of clothes", were collected from the station and taken to Mickleover by motor car. They were to be the guests of Mr Preston Jones who had provided two furnished cottages on his Mickleover House estate. For two families it was a lifeline. But it was a very small drop in the ocean in what was to become a complex absorption as almost a quarter of a million of their compatriots fled to Britain.

〜〜〜〜〜〜〜〜〜〜〜〜〜〜〜

IN November 1914, an advertisement appeared in the *Evening Telegraph* asking for contributions of warm clothing. Lady Inglefield of Windley, the wife of a senior admiral, helped spearhead the campaign. She wanted: "Jerseys, Helmets and Mittens in Navy Blue Wool, also Socks, for the crews of the vessels of the Royal Naval Motor-boat Reserve. All parcels to be sent to Mickleover Manor, Derby."

〜〜〜〜〜〜〜〜〜〜〜〜〜〜〜

ALTHOUGH something more often associated with a later conflict, during the Great War Mickleover had its own Home Guard. In June 1915 the detachment was inspected for the first time, by the Earl of Harrington from Melbourne Hall. The following month there was another inspection, this time by Admiral Sir Frederick Inglefield (who would later be a member of the official inquiry into the loss of RMS *Lusitania*, a maritime tragedy that influenced the decision of the United States to declare war in 1917). This time, there was a church service at which the Mickleover Home Guard were thanked for their efforts by the Rev R. C. Bindley, who noted that the uniforms they were about to take up would symbolise "self-sacrifice, obedience and trust in God".

〜〜〜〜〜〜〜〜〜〜〜〜〜〜〜

IN June 1915, Thomas Radford, a farmer of Ivy Farm, Mickleover, was summoned to the Derby Borough Police Court for selling milk "which was not of the nature and substance demanded". Four samples of milk tested appeared to show that water had been added. The defence argued that natural variations in the milk provided by cows, and regulations on the minimum content of fat and non-fatty solids, meant that some milk, in the state it came from the cow, would have tested as sub-standard. The prosecution argued that the levels that had been found could not have been possible in unadulterated milk. Mr Radford argued that he fed his cattle very well but that the milk produced in April – the period during which the samples had been taken – had not been of such a high quality as that produced in May. The bench retired to consider their verdicts and ruled that in two of the cases the milk was below standard. They imposed a fine of 20s on each instance.

~~~~~~

AFTER the war A. Preston Jones of Mickleover House brought to the village a building that would be known as the Memorial Hut. It had previously been used by the YMCA at Derby LMS

Volunteers gather ready to re-erect the Memorial Hut after the Great War.

station to serve refreshments to soldiers on their way to and from the fighting. In Mickleover it was to become a hub of local activities, before eventually being converted to use as the village library. It stands today in Station Road and is hired out to local groups, almost 100 years after it served the needs of local troops.

THREE Mickleover brothers, whose parents lived in The Square, were all killed, two of them within weeks of each other. Herbert Dunn, of the Leicestershire Regiment, was killed in action at Delville Wood on the Somme in July 1916. George Dunn, who was awarded the Military Medal while serving with the Grenadier Guards, died of his wounds in September 1916 after being injured during the Battle of the Somme. Thomas Dunn, who was with the Sherwood Foresters, was killed in action at Pilckem Ridge in the Ypres salient in July 1917. The bodies of Thomas and Herbert have no known grave.

Not every local casualty fell on the battlefield. In December 1914, Lawrence Victor Ball of Station Road, Mickleover, died in the Derbyshire Royal Infirmary. He had only recently joined up, and was a private in the 5th Sherwood Foresters (Sherwood Foresters) stationed at Swanwick. When he enlisted, Ball had been in good health, except for what appeared to be slight trouble with one ear.

Before long a military doctor sent him home, suspecting influenza. Private Ball was eventually admitted to the DRI suffering with "terrible pains in the head". He was operated upon, but died in the operating theatre when his "respiration changed". An inquest ruled that he had perished from meningitis, secondary to the ear trouble.

In contrast, his brother, Harry, was killed in action in the last year of the war. Harry, a medic attached the Gordon Highlanders, was, like Victor, born in Mickleover but spent part of his childhood in Allestree. Before joining the Army he had been employed as an asylum attendant. He was awarded the Military Medal.

Brothers Arthur and Robert Milward, sons of the late William and Martha Millward of Common End Farm, Mickleover, were killed within four months of each other in 1917.

At least two other Mickleover brothers died while serving of their country around this time. Charles Lawson was killed in action in 1916, during the Battle of Flers-Courcelette, a subsidiary attack of the Battle of the Somme. His sailor brother, Percy, died in August 1919.

————

Lest We Forget
World War One Casualties with Mickleover connections

GEORGE WILLIAM ADAMS
Sergeant, 16th Battalion, Sherwood Foresters
Died 10 October 1916, aged 25
Son of George and Sarah Adams of Station Road, Mickleover
Buried at Mill Road Cemetery, Thiepval, France

CHARLES AYRE
Gunner, 1st Reserve Brigade, Royal Field Artillery
Died in the UK, 13 June 1915, aged 32
Son of Henry and Christiana Ayre of The Limes, Mickleover
Buried at Mickleover (All Saints) Churchyard

H. HARRY BALL MM
Sergeant, Royal Army Medical Corps attached 1st Battalion, Gordon Highlanders
Died 28 March 1918, aged 32
Commemorated on the Arras Memorial

LAWRENCE VICTOR BALL
Private, 5th Reserve Battalion, Sherwood Foresters
Died in Derby, 4 December 1914, aged 24
Buried at Mickleover (All Saints') Churchyard

ROBERT VINCENT BEARE

Lance Corporal, 2nd Battalion, Worcestershire Regiment
Died 29 September 1918, aged 41
Son of John and Sarah Beare of Mickleover
Buried at Pigeon-Ravine Cemetery, Epehy, France

ARTHUR HENRY BUSH

Sergeant, "D" Squadron, Derbyshire Yeomanry
Died 22 August 1915, aged 26
Son of Arthur and Jennie Bush of Staker House, Mickleover
Commemorated on the Helles Memorial, Gallipoli Peninsula

ARTHUR HENRY CABORN

Private, 10th Battalion, King's Own Yorkshire Light Infantry
Died 9 April 1917, aged 26
Son of Joseph and Jane Caborn of Common End, Mickleover,
Derby.
Buried at Cojeul British Cemetery, St. Martin sur Cojeul, France

WILLIAM HUGH COXON

Second Lieutenant, 3rd Battalion, Sherwood Foresters
Died 11 March 1915, aged 21
Commemorated on the Le Touret Memorial

GEORGE WILLIAM DUNN MM

Acting Company Sergeant Major, 3rd Battalion, Grenadier
Guards
Died 18 September 1916, aged 30
Son of Herbert William and Emma Dunn of The Square,
Mickleover; husband of Lucy Dunn, of 78 Franchise Street,
Derby
Buried at Grove Town Cemetery, Meaulte, France

THOMAS DUNN

Company Sergeant Major, 1st Battalion, Sherwood Foresters
Died 31 July 1917, aged 28
Son of Herbert William and Emma Dunn of The Square, Mickleover; husband of Florence Dunn, of 7, South Drive, New Town, Hebburn-on-Tyne
Commemorated on the Ypres (Menin Gate) Memorial

HERBERT ARTHUR DUNN

Lance Corporal, 8th Battalion, Leicestershire Regiment
Died 15 July 1916, aged 24
Son of Herbert William and Emma Dunn of The Square, Mickleover; husband of Rebecca Dunn, of 17, Chapel Rd., Grassmoor, Chesterfield
Commemorated on the Thiepval Memorial

ERIC WILLIAM DUNSTAN

Private, "A" Company, 2nd/5th Battalion, Sherwood Foresters
Died 9 September 1918, aged 25
Son of William Edward and Fanny Dunstan of Cattle Hill
Buried at Le Quesnoy Communal Cemetery, France

ARTHUR FOSTER

Private, 2nd/7th Battalion, Sherwood Foresters
Died 21 March 1918, aged 31
Son of Ann Foster and the late William Foster of Ash Cottage, Goosecroft Lane, Mickleover
Commemorated on the Arras Memorial

ARTHUR WILLIAM FOSTER

Lance Corporal, 10th Battalion, Sherwood Foresters
Died 13 October 1917, aged 30
Commemorated on the Tyne Cot Memorial

ERNEST FOSTER

Private, 2nd/7th Battalion, Sherwood Foresters
Died 21 March 1918, aged 19
Son of James and Fanny Foster of The Hollow, Mickleover
Commemorated on the Arras Memorial

PERCY JOHN FOSTER

Corporal, 46th Division Ammunition Column, Royal Field
Artillery, posted to "Z", 46th Trench Mortar Battery, Royal
Field Artillery
Died 22 October 1917, aged 25
Husband of Edith Foster of 2 Hinds Yard, Mickleover (later
Westbury Street, Derby)
Commemorated on the Loos Memorial

THOMAS HAYDN FOSTER

Private, 1st Battalion, Sherwood Foresters
Died 4 March 1917, aged 28
Buried at Hem Farm Military Cemetery, Hem-Monacu, France

HERBERT WILLIAM HAINES

Private, 16th Battalion, Sherwood Foresters
Died 3 August 1917, aged 19
Son of William and Mary Haines of Mickleover
Buried at Brandhoek New Military Cemetery No3, Belgium

ROBERT HENRY HIGGINS

Private, King's Shropshire Light Infantry, then 423rd Area
Employment Company, Labour Corps
Died 3 November 1918, aged 29
Husband of Florence Higgins of Common End
Buried at Mickleover (All Saints') Churchyard

WILLIAM MACHAM

Private, 6th/7th Battalion, Royal Scots Fusiliers
Died 27 April 1918, aged 27
Son of Charles and Emma Macham; husband of Amy Macham
of 5 Station Road, Mickleover
Buried at Denain Communal Cemetery, France

ARTHUR MILLWARD

Private, 2nd Battalion, Sherwood Foresters
Died 8 March 1917, aged 41
Son of the late William and Martha Millward of Common End
Farm, Mickleover
Buried at Etaples Military Cemetery, France

ROBERT ERNEST MILLWARD

Private, 2nd Battalion, Sherwood Foresters
Died 1 July 1917, aged 29
Son of the late William and Martha Millward of Common End
Farm, Mickleover
Commemorated on the Loos Memorial

ALBERT VICTOR ORME

Private, Derbyshire Yeomanry
Died 20 August 1915, aged 23
Son of William and Mary Orme of Woodbine Cottage,
Mickleover
Commemorated on the Helles Memorial, Turkey

DAVID OUTRAM

Private, 1st/8th Battalion, Durham Light Infantry
Died 27 May 1918, aged 18
Commemorated on the Soissons Memorial

CHARLES THOMAS RAWSON

Rifleman, 18th Battalion, King's Royal Rifle Corps
Died 15 September 1916, aged 21
Son of Thomas Wigley Rawson, house painter
Commemorated on the Thiepval Memorial

PERCY WILLIAM RAWSON

Able Seaman, Bristol Z/4724, Royal Naval Volunteer Reserve
Died 21 August 1919 aged 22
Son of Thomas Wigley Rawson, house painter
Buried at Mickleover (All Saints') Churchyard

WILLIAM ALBERT SHARDLOW

Private, 7th Battalion, North Staffordshire Regiment
Died 31 August 1918, aged 25
Son of Albert and Emma Shardlow of Mickleover (and later 72
Woods Lane, Derby)
Commemorated on the Tehran Memorial, Iran

WILLIAM ALFRED THOMPSON

Gunner, "D" Battery, 230th Brigade, Royal Field Artillery
Died 26 April 1918, aged 21
Son of William and Rosehannah Thompson, Hullock's Yard,
Cattle Hill, Mickleover
Buried at Fouquieres Churchyard Extension, France

EDMUND TOWNEND

Rifleman, 9th Battalion, Rifle Brigade
Died 15 September 1916, aged 19
Resided in Mickleover
Commemorated on the Thiepval Memorial

ARTHUR WAINWRIGHT

Private, 10th Battalion, Sherwood Foresters
Died 20 August, 1918 aged 22
Son of Charles and Rose Wainwright of Western Road, Mickleover
Buried at St. Sever Cemetery Extension, Rouen, France

JOHN FREDERICK WALTERS

Private, 1st Battalion, Royal Scots Fusiliers
Died 10 June 1918, aged 35
Son of John and Elizabeth Walters; husband of Edith Mary Walters, of 72 Peartree Street, Derby
Buried at Pernes British Cemetery, France

BENJAMIN TREVOR WIBBERLEY

Corporal, 3rd Battalion, King's Royal Rifle Corps
Died 3 November 1918, aged 23
Son of Alfred and Maria Wibberley of Mickleover
Buried at Mikra British Cemetery, Kalamaria, Greece

SAMUEL WINFIELD

Private, Derbyshire Yeomanry
Died 21 August 1915, aged 19
Son of Samuel and Esther Winfield of Station Road, Mickleover
Commemorated on the Helles Memorial, Gallipoli Peninsula

GEORGE S. YATES

Lance Corporal, 3rd Battalion, King's Royal Rife Corps
Died 19 May 1915, aged 28
Son of George and Louisa Yates of 3 Camden Street, Derby; a native of Mickleover
Buried at Bailleul Communal Cemetery Extension (Nord), France

*The former home of the Mickleover branch of the
Royal British Legion on Western Road.*

Visiting the battlefields of the Great War is popular today, but as far back as 1937, even as Europe headed towards another conflict, members of Mickleover branch of the British Legion (the "Royal" wasn't added until 1971) announced that they were planning a tour of Great War battlefields. The trip was planned for 1939. Mr R. Webster, chairman of the executive committee, said it was hoped that all ex-servicemen in Mickleover and district would support the branch. Mr T. Radford congratulated the Legion, telling them: "You know what won the war? British self-sacrifice, British endurance and British perseverance. If you want to make the Mickleover branch a success, all you have to do is to employ those same qualities in your activities."

The new RBL premises, fit for the 21st century.

18
Mickleover at War
1939-1945

AS Adolf Hitler's Nazi ambitions reached out across mainland Europe, many Britons feared another conflict. With the horrors of the Great War still casting a terrible dark shadow over the land, in every city, town and village plans were afoot, to bolster defences and prepare for another conflict. The village of Mickleover was no exception.

In 1937, as tensions in Europe rose, Repton Rural Council sent to Mickleover a document outlining what preparations ought to be made for precautions against air-raids. Mickleover representative Mr W. H. Young was concerned that "there was hardly a paragraph in the memorandum which did not leave a question of doubt" and that the scheme was far too detailed for a village like Mickleover.

He felt the whole thing was very premature and that "if we were to take the scheme as laid down, very likely we should find ourselves doing a lot of work which, later, we should be told was unnecessary."

The Parish Council, though, agreed to do "all it could to co-operate in the matter". One Mr Hufton determined that there was "nothing more certain than we have to make some provision against gas attack. Some method of warning at least, is necessary".

It was generally feared that as well as the proposed aerodrome at Burnaston, the County Mental Hospital might be targeted for attack. In the end it was decided to organise meetings so that the public could be instructed in what to do in case of a gas attack and to teach them general first-aid skills.

By March 1938, the entire Parish Council, as well as representatives of local organisations, was elected to serve on the Air-Raid Precaution Committee. The Home Office had promised to cover 70 per cent of the costs of its "approved expenditure", although what would count as "approved" was unclear. According to the committee, arrangements had already been made for a siren to be fixed on a local garage: "Volunteers would be required as air-wardens for every street, road and lane in the parish. Fire squads, life-saving squads and a contingent of workers of both sexes would also be required."

It was also decided to look into buying a small fire engine for Mickleover, which it was believed could be done for as little as £165. This would cost ratepayers a "penny rate". Since the next rate would show a reduction of 2d, it would be possible to take this and still reduce the levy.

By May 1938, so many schemes for protecting the Mickleover public had been advanced that Mr Hufton felt this had resulted in "general apathy from locals".

In October that year, the first respirators, now commonly known as gas masks, were available for Mickleover residents. Several thousand were taken to the Council Schools on Uttoxeter Road and, under the watchful eyes of Chief Warden Mr A. Campbell and his deputy, Mr F, Bailey, dutiful locals collected some 3,232. The remainder was to be given to the appointed wardens who would each be responsible for distributing them in their various sectors.

It was also agreed that it was now time to plan further measures, such as the provision of trenches, bomb-proof shelters, wardens' posts and first-aid posts. Already more than 100 volunteers had been enrolled for ARP work in the village.

Evacuees

WHEN war against Germany was finally declared in September 1939, the village anticipated its first refugees. Under the headline "Mickleover Waits" the *Derby Evening Telegraph* reported that, although the folk of Mickleover had been told to expect as many as 650 youngsters and their mothers – evacuees from Birmingham – they might not arrive at all. It seemed the anticipated number of willing evacuees had been over-estimated. However, "helpers at Mickleover should stand by in case their services are needed".

Those first evacuees did eventually arrive, followed by several hundred more, and in July 1940, the Ministry of Health told locals to expect a further 1,500. While sympathy for their plight was almost universal, it seemed that some locals had not taken to their new guests with quite such ease. Some parishioners within RRC had resolved not to take any more evacuees from Birmingham at all.

According to the *Evening* Telegraph one Mickleover resident, Mr F. T. Emery, commented that "parents from Birmingham visited their children already in the district regularly at the weekends and that they took advantage of the hospitality of householders without as much as a thank-you".

There was a rumour that, in one case, a fully clothed child that had been taken out by its parents was returned "in rags".

It seemed that "children from farther afield" would be more welcome, but all objections were overruled and Mickleover organisers were told that billeting officers "could use their own discretion in the placing of children in homes". Mr T. Radford, the member for Mickleover, noted that if 1,500 children were sent to Mickleover, there would be little discretion to use.

Some of the children too were very unhappy about their situation. In September 1944, one 11-year-old London girl, staying in the village with her mother, took matters into her own hands when she set a fire at her wartime billet at 191 Western Road. She was summoned to court accused of causing £75-worth of damage by setting fire to a table runner, a bedspread and a curtain, as well as other attempts in the days leading up to the incident. It seemed the young girl simply wanted her mother to take her home. The court was sympathetic, the case was dismissed and the girl and her mother had to pay 16s in costs.

Some young Mickleover residents had themselves been evacuated to a safer place. For young Hilary and Alan Verdon, whose parents lived in Western Road, that refuge had been a long way away. The siblings had been sent to Bloemfontein in South Africa in 1940 and, in December 1943, the *Evening Telegraph* reported that they had received a radio message from their parents via the *Hello Children* programme broadcast in the South African service.

The First Casualty

AS far removed from the industrial centre of Derby as Mickleover might have seemed, it did not escape the attentions of the Luftwaffe. Indeed it was a Mickleover resident, one Elsie May Henson, who was to become the first mortally wounded victim of bombing in the Derby area. On 2 July 1940, the day that the *Derby Evening Telegraph* reported the sinking of four Italian submarines in the Mediterranean, the same newspaper carried a small item about the death in hospital of Mrs Henson, who had died as a result of injuries sustained during an air raid on "a Midlands town" in the early hours of 25 June.

Houses on Jackson Avenue were severely damaged
during the air-raid of August 1940.

Although wartime censorship would not allow Mrs Henson's local paper to reveal it, that Midlands town was Derby and she had been fleeing her house at 22 Jackson Avenue when she had been hit in the chest by splinters of a bomb that had fallen into her neighbours' rose-bed. The 39-year-old's husband and their seven-year-old daughter, Hazel, had been in the house at the time. Remarkably, although the house was substantially damaged, neither suffered any wounds.

Mr Henson told the *Evening Telegraph*: "When I was on the stairs there was a crash and the house was filled with black smoke. For a moment I was stunned and it was all I could do to grope my way out of the house. I hardly knew what I was doing. On reaching the garden I saw my wife lying at the entrance to the shelter."

Neighbours quickly came to their aid and, while one turned off the gas and electricity supply to surrounding homes, the Hensons' near neighbour, Mr G. S. Bradford, an ARP first-aider, went to help and decided to take the injured woman to hospital

A police officer inspects damage at 22 Jackson Avenue, where in 1940 Mrs Elsie Henson became Derby's first mortally wounded civilian victim of bombing in the Second World War.

in his car. However, the blast had partially collapsed his garage and he had to "crash the car through the woodwork to get it on the road". Mr Bradford also said that every door of his own house had been blown from its hinges. Indeed, in his scramble to get out, he had gashed his forehead and later had to be treated at his own first-aid post.

Next door to the Hensons lived the Coopers, whose home was reduced "almost to wreckage". Mr Cooper, carrying their baby, and his wife had been coming down the stairs at the time of the impact.

"There was a blinding flash. The house seemed to rock on its foundations, then settled back. Debris from walls and ceilings flew about, but we came out unharmed … we saw that a crater had been made where my rose-bed used to be."

Some distance away, three LDV (later Home Guard) volunteers, on duty for the first time, took shelter in large iron pipes as they lay in a field and reported that splinters and shrapnel bounced against the outside of the pipes.

Elsie Henson's short fight for life meant that she was not the first fatality in Derby's war. Elizabeth Evans of Violet Street in Pear Tree, although injured after Mrs Henson, sustained wounds that proved immediately fatal.

Raising Funds – and Morale

FUND-raising during wartime was vital – and popular. In November 1942, the Huffin Heath Fire Watching Group held a whist drive at Mickleover Golf Club House and raised seven guineas (£7.35) for the Merchant Navy Comforts Service Fund.

Wartime also provided plenty of opportunity to meet new people. In September 1940, the *Derby Evening Telegraph* reported that the Nag's Head had played host to some 80 soldiers and a similar number of Derby shop girls, as well as to WAAFs and ATS women, at a tea dance. A Royal Army Service Corps unit band provided the music and there was a special cabaret. It was quite an occasion, with the Mayor, Alderman A. T. Neal, telling the paper: "Immediately one entered the hall a feeling of being at home was experienced."

Following one dance in the village, in February 1942, there was unexpected drama. Nineteeen-year-old Austrian, Heinz Hoffman, who, with the help of the Quakers, had fled to Britain in 1939 with his parents, was arrested. As an "alien", Hoffman was required to register and to abide by a curfew that required him to be in his place of residence – Hill Farm, Kirk Langley, where he was a labourer – between 10.30pm and 6am. However, the temptation to attend a dance in Mickleover had proved too much and when he was approached by two police officers, it was 2.15am. To compound his troubles, he had to confess that did not have his registration documents to hand. At a court hearing the following month it was revealed that Hoffman had previously been sentenced for a similar offence.

Thanks to a strong plea by his solicitor, who stated that while Hoffman might have been "a silly ass" he was a "willing and most conscientious worker", the teenager avoided a prison sentence and was fined 10s for absenting himself from his place of residence during his curfew and an additional 10s for failing to produce his documentation.

IN November 1942, a 9pm curfew of buses and trolley services was introduced in the Derby area. On Sundays there would be no trolley buses before 1pm and no motor buses until 2pm. Bus users, particularly those living in the outlying areas like Mickleover, were asked not to wait until the last bus.

FOR the Ayre family of the The Limes, the war was a particularly worrying time. In June 1940 their young son, Lt Charles Ayre of the Sherwood Foresters, was taken prisoner at Eichstatt in Bavaria. Two years later, his older brother, Lt Peter Phips Ayre of the Royal Corps of Signals, was also captured. He was held at Weinsberg, Baden Wurttemberg. In June 1944 the *Evening Telegraph* reported: "A message broadcast from a German source states that Lt Peter Ayre ... is keeping fit and well."

IN May 1943, Trent Motor Traction's first gas-powered bus ran on the Mickleover route. The double-decker bus was fitted with a gas-producer trailer unit and was the first of some 30 vehicles that Trent was to convert under a Ministry of Transport scheme. Gas vehicles were suitable only for use in the less hilly districts. A little petrol was required to ensure that the bus could keep to its timetable, but gas buses were smoother running and much quieter.

AS the war drew on, stricter rationing rules were introduced. In June 1943, more than 4,000 new ration books and identity cards were distributed from the Memorial Hut in Mickleover. Forty clerks and helpers, some from the QVS and British Legion, ensured that there were no queues.

WHILE many Mickleover folk were required to help with war work, not everyone found the discipline and routine easy to accept. Twenty-year-old Doris Udall of The Green was an aircraft worker but was required by the Ministry of Labour to do first-aid work as an unpaid Civil Defence worker. In October 1943, she appeared at Derby County Police Court for failing to carry out her duty and for being absent from her post on three separate days. She claimed that, on two of these occasions, she had been detained at work. She pleaded guilty and was fined £6.

THERE was much emphasis on "growing your own" and in increasing production from local farms. It was a great success. In November 1943, Rough Heanor Farm was awarded "first prize for root crops" from the Derbyshire War Agricultural Committee. The farm had previously fallen into a such a "terrible state" before the Mental Hospital Committee had taken it over, that the War Agricultural Committee had considered taking control. Now, under the eye of Mr H. S. Fitch as bailiff, "with some technical knowledge, and ... his untiring efforts, it has rapidly become a model farm".

EVEN out in the sticks, the blackout was strictly enforced, even once the threat of air-raids had decreased. The *Evening Telegraph* listed the name and addresses of those who had broken the regulations. In April 1944, Dorothy Harrison of 55 Jackson Avenue was fined 15s at Derby County Police Court for "showing a light".

SOME Mickleover residents were hauled up before the authorities for less war-related infractions. One, unnamed, Mickleover resident was the subject of some debate when he was found to be visiting an allotment in Littleover, cutting out a square of turf and taking it back to his home in Mickleover. It seemed the gentleman concerned was already well on the way to making a nice lawn for his garden. However, he was instructed to return the turf.

BY the end of June 1944 the news from the battlefront was good. The invasion of Normandy was going well. But for one Mickleover family there was still concern. Eighteen-year-old Lance-Corporal Hubert Hufton, a Commando, was in an English hospital recovering from his injuries. He had been part of the first wave on D-Day and had written to his parents, Mr and Mrs C. L. Hufton of 24 Station Road, to tell them of a week's fierce fighting before he was put out of action by a sniper's bullet in his back.

IN late 1944 it was decided that a temporary part-time fire station in Mickleover would close, as the district would now come under the protection of the Derby National Fire Service. It was agreed that the NFS would keep the tenancy on the Mickleover site until peacetime, at which point a retained fire brigade would, once again, be formed. This proved somewhat contentious because, as Repton Rural District Council clerk Mr F. Bailey pointed out, a 1938 Act and a 1939 Home Office communication had both insisted that Mickleover have a fire station in peacetime and it was odd that "during war time it was apparently not required". There was also concern at the length of time it would take for the fire engines from Derby to reach Mickleover. Fire force commander A. A. I. Galloway estimated it would take "seven or eight minutes" to reach the top of Station Road and offered to make a surprise test for the council at any time to back up his estimate.

~~~~~~~~~~~~~~~~~~

IN November 1944, a seemingly minor collision resulted in tragic consequences. While travelling along Uttoxeter Road, a Trent double-decker bus received what the *Evening Telegraph* reported was a "glancing blow on the front wheel" from a lorry that was on the opposite side of the road. The blow caused the bus to overturn. One man, Hugh Munro of The Green, was killed and 26 of the 45 passengers were injured. Thirteen of them were admitted to hospital, nine to the nearby City Hospital and four to the Derbyshire Royal Infirmary. Two days after the accident, while most of the injured were improving, others were described as "ill after a poor night" and "rather ill".

The lorry driver, who worked for a Nottingham haulage company, told police that, although he remembered passing the bus, he was unaware of any impact. He had later discovered that the tyre of one the offside wheels was flat and the rim buckled.

"Until I read in a Derby newspaper the next day that a bus had overturned at Mickleover, I knew nothing about it ... I began to wonder if I had been involved," the driver told the coroner at Mr Munro's inquest.

Bus driver William Thornhill stated: "The steering wheel was spun around and I lost control of it. The bus swerved across the road on to the footpath and overturned. I broke the glass of my cab to get out and assist the passengers."

Harold Milward of Etwall Road, who had been a passenger, testified: "I felt an impact; I heard a slight grazing noise. The next thing I knew the 'bus was going over."

The coroner's inquiry into the incident ruled that it was nothing more than a "very tragic accident". Even in wartime, it seemed, the perils of everyday life could strike a tragic blow.

WHEN the war in Europe ended on 8 May 1945, plans were drawn up for a victory parade in Mickleover. On Sunday, 13 May, contingents from every military service took part in a march from the Memorial Hut on Station Road to All Saints' Church, where there was held a thanksgiving service.

IT was quite a shock for Britons when, hard upon the heels of Victory in Europe, came news that food rationing was to become even stricter. So disappointed was Western Road resident R. T. Howells with the news that the ration was to be cut further, that they put pen to paper and wrote to the *Evening Telegraph* to complain:

> "May I, on behalf of thousands of housewives, strongly protest against the cut in the food rations? After many months of trying to vary the daily meals on wartime food, many people must be asking themselves whether we have won or lost the European War. Had Germany won the war can one suppose that she would have cut her food rations? What about it, housewives?"

WHEN it came to fund-raising after the war, it seemed that the people of Mickleover weren't considered to be pulling their weight. The *Derby Evening Telegraph* of 25 October 1945 called "Muckle More Please, Mickleover!" While Repton Rural District's Thanksgiving Week target of £100,000 has now been exceeded, "savers in Mickleover must look to their laurels." Given a parish target of £15,000, they had managed only £872.

IN 1945, one Mickleover businessman found himself in a sticky mess after getting caught up in a large-scale scam. Since 1919, trade in a host of vital products, among them linseed oil, had required a licence. In October 1945, ten men were taken to court for dealing in the essential substance without a licence. Linseed oil had a variety of uses, including providing a base for many paints. Charles Ayre of The Limes, who was a director of a varnish and colour manufactory, stood accused of purchasing the product without the required licence. The court case revealed that the linseed oil had been stolen from London and had been illegally distributed to a number of British towns and cities. Although the Derby merchant who had sold on the linseed oil pleaded not guilty, Mr Ayre pleaded guilty to the offence and was fined £250 with £75 costs.

Lest We Forget
World War Two Casualties with Mickleover connections

LESLIE GEORGE BENTLEY
Sergeant, 100 Squadron, RAF Volunteer Reserve
Died 28 July 1943
Commemorated on the Runnymede Memorial, Surrey

THOMAS ALFRED BODEN

Gunner, Royal Artillery
Died 29 October 1940, aged 31
Son of Mrs E. Boden and the late Mr Boden of Mickleover
Died in a military hospital. Buried at Mickleover (All Saints')
Churchyard

GEOFFREY BOOTH

Flying Officer (Air Gunner), 103 Squadron, RAF
Died 26 November 1943, aged 25
Son of Harold and Beatrice Booth of Mickleover; husband of
Doreen Isabel Booth
Buried at Berlin 1939-1945 War Cemetery

SIDNEY BRADLEY

Sergeant (Air Gunner), 206 Squadron, RAF Volunteer Reserve
Died 19 November 1940, aged 24
Son of Cecil Charles Sidney and Ethel Selina Bradley. Husband
of Kathleen Bradley of Littleover
Buried at Mickleover (All Saints') Churchyard

HAROLD BURGESS

Able Seaman, D/JX, HMS President III, Royal Navy
Died 2 November 1942, aged 28
Son of Mr. and Mrs. J. H. Burgess of Mickleover
Commemorated on the Plymouth Naval Memorial, Devon

HAROLD EDWIN CLARKE

Private, Royal Army Ordnance Corps
Died 17 June 1940, aged 24
Son of Thomas Edwin and Edith Annie Clarke of Mickleover
Buried at Prefailles Communal Cemetery, France

FREDERICK COTTINGTON

Sapper, 1000 Docks Maintenance Company, Royal Engineers
Died 2 March 1943, aged 22
Son of Sidney Thomas and Alice Louisa Cottington of Mickleover
Buried at Tripoli War Cemetery, Libya

JOHN ROBERT DAWSON

Sergeant (Wireless Operator/Air Gunner), 97 Squadron, RAF Volunteer Reserve
Died 5 October 1942, aged 27
Son of Frederick and Nellie Dawson. Husband of Bertha Dawson of Mickleover
Buried at Jonkerbos War Cemetery, Netherlands

EDGAR DOLPHIN

Sergeant, 7 Squadron, RAF Volunteer Reserve
Died 13 July 1942, aged 25
Buried Biddulph (St Lawrence) Churchyard

DOUGLAS RONALD GREENUP

Flight Lieutenant (Pilot), RAF
Died 30 March 1943.
Husband of Marie Greenup of Mickleover
Buried at Littleover Churchyard

JONATHAN ALLEN JAMES

Signalman, Royal Corps of Signals
Died 5 April 1945, aged 29
Son of George Allen and Anne Gaines James of Mickleover
Buried at Berlin 1939-1945 War Cemetery, Germany

WILLIAM FRANK LANGSTON

Private, 1/5th Battalion, Queen's Royal Regiment
Died 23 November 1944, aged 22
Buried at Mook War Cemetery, Netherlands

MAURICE RUPERT MOORLEY

Flying Officer (Pilot Instructor), RAF Volunteer Reserve
Died 10 September 1942, aged 29
Son of Charles and Lucy Moorley of 329 Uttoxeter Road,
Mickleover; husband of Catherine J. E. Moorley of Nuthall,
Nottinghamshire.
Buried at Mickleover (All Saints') Churchyard

LEONARD GRANVILLE MOSELEY

Sergeant (Flight Engineer), 51 Squadron, RAF Volunteer
Reserve
Died 8 February 1943, aged 23
Son of William Harlow Moseley and Sarah Moseley of
Mickleover
Buried at Mickleover (All Saints') Churchyard

KENNETH EDWIN PEAKE

Sergeant (Air Gunner), 514 Squadron, RAF Volunteer Reserve
Died 16 March 1944
Buried at Villars-le-Pautel Communal Cemetery, France

MALCOLM SCHOFIELD SMITH

Pilot Officer (Pilot), RAF Volunteer Reserve
Died 4 May 1941, aged 24
Son of Captain Alfred Leopold and Ethel F. S. Smith of
Mickleover
Buried at Mickleover (All Saints') Churchyard

CHARLES JAMES STORER

Sergeant (Wireless Operator /Air Gunner), 78 Squadron, RAF
Volunteer Reserve
Died 7 September 1941, aged 30
Buried at Tietjerksteradeel (Bergum) Protestant Churchyard,
Netherlands

FREDERICK VICTOR THORNHILL

Sapper, 291 Army Troops Company, Royal Engineers
Died 21 May 1940, aged 21
Buried at Morville sur Andelle Churchyard, France

ROY THOMPSON

Sergeant, 7 Squadron, RAF Volunteer Reserve
Died 22 May 1944
Commemorated on the Runnymede Memorial, Surrey

ALBERT WARNER

Ordinary Seaman, HM Submarine P33, Royal Navy
Died 20 August 1941, aged 24
Son of Albert Victor and Eleanor Alice Warner of Mickleover
Lost when P33 was sunk in the Mediterranean. Commemorated
on the Chatham Naval Memorial, Kent

KENNETH ALFRED WESLEY

Private, 2nd Battalion, Royal Warwickshire Regiment
21 July 1944, aged 29.
Son of Mr and Mrs Wesley of Mickleover; husband of Sylvia
Dorothy Wesley of Derby
Buried at La Delivrande War Cemetery, Douvres, Calvados,
Normandy, France

HARVEY WILLIAM WRIGHT

Sergeant (Pilot), 110 Squadron, RAF Volunteer Reserve
Died 18 April 1941, aged 24
Son of George and Sarah M. Wright of Mickleover
Buried at Mickleover (All Saints') Churchyard

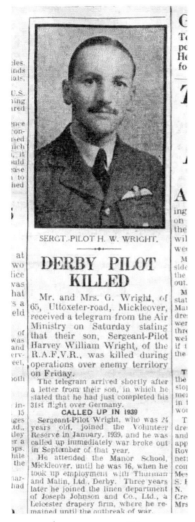

SERGT.-PILOT H. W. WRIGHT.

DERBY PILOT KILLED

Mr. and Mrs. G. Wright, of 65, Uttoxeter-road, Mickleover, received a telegram from the Air Ministry on Saturday stating that their son, Sergeant-Pilot Harvey William Wright, of the R.A.F.V.R., was killed during operations over enemy territory on Friday.

The telegram arrived shortly after a letter from their son, in which he stated that he had just completed his 31st flight over Germany.

CALLED UP IN 1939

Sergeant-Pilot Wright, who was 24 years old, joined the Volunteer Reserve in January, 1939, and he was called up immediately war broke out in September of that year.

He attended the Manor School, Mickleover, until he was 16, when he took up employment with Thurman and Malin, Ltd., Derby. Three years later he joined the linen department of Joseph Johnson and Co., Ltd., a Leicester drapery firm, where he remained until the outbreak of war.

A newspaper cutting announcing the death of Sgt-Pilot Harvey Wright.

Mickleover's War Memorial stands in the grounds of All Saints' Church.

19
This 'n' That

ONE Sunday evening in 1830, residents in Mickleover were fortunate enough to see "that rare phenomenon, the Lunar Rainbow". Just as the sun can reveal a rainbow during the day, a very bright moon can do the same at night. But such a "moonbow" is very rare because the Moon needs to be full, or almost full, there needs to be a clear sky in front of the Moon but rain to the opposite side of the sky, the sky must be very dark and the Moon itself must be no more than 42 degrees above the horizon.

The *Derby Mercury* noted that the lunar rainbow was "beautifully visible … the colours were perfectly and distinctly defined, and their brilliancy was such, as to be reflected in a second Bow, or rather shadow. It appeared to be at the distance of a few hundred yards and was visible for many minutes. The sky around it presented an extraordinary luminous appearance."

IN 1838, a rather puzzling marriage took place. The banns of Miss Steer of Mickleover and her betrothed, Thomas Cox of Burton, had been read at St Werburgh's Church in Derby, both having connections with that parish. On 13 April the couple "presented themselves" to the minister there, and were married. The newly-weds left the church "to ruminate on the solemnity of its marriage service" when another couple entered and "to the great astonishment of the minister demanded that he would marry them, stating who they were" – the real Mr Cox and Miss Steer. The minister told them that either he had "just concluded marrying them, or that they could not be the above-mentioned parties". Not only that, because he had just married "Mr Cox and Miss Steer" the banns for that union had just expired. The couple, unsurprisingly, were extremely unhappy and demanded that the ceremony go ahead. The minister was adamant – he simply could not marry two couples with the same banns. Their only option was to leave the church and buy a licence, by which they were married at the same church the following day.

Not only had the couple been "robbed" of their special day, their half-crown costs for publishing the banns had been wasted and they also had to pay for a special licence.

~~~~~~~~~~~~~~~~~~~~~~~~~~~~~~~~~~~~

IN September 1842, a rather worrying discovery was made in Mickleover – a live locust. As it transpired, Mickleover was just one place in which a specimen of *Gryllus Migratorius*, or Asiatic locust had been found in recent weeks. Previously there had been finds at Chesterfield and at Sheffield. Some time later a fourth insect was found near Burton upon Trent and was believed to have been "ready to deposit" its "40 to 50 eggs".

~~~~~~~~~~~~~~~~~~~~~~~~~~~~~~~~~~~~

Derby Mercury, 11 October 1865
"Lost, in Derby, on September 11th, a small PAPER PARCEL, containing a Book supposed to have been left in a cab from the Railway Station. The Parcel directed to Miss Powys, Ladies Waiting Room, Derby Station – Whoever will bring the same to the Lodge, Mickleover, will be rewarded"

~~~~~~~~~~~~~~~~~~~~~~~~~~~~~~~~~~~~

IN 1874, Mickleover opened a convalescent home with the following advertisement: "Mickleover Convalescent Home for Invalids, or persons requiring rest and country air, will be opened June 1st. All letters to be addressed the 'Matron', Convalescent Home, Mickleover."

IN August 1880, the *Derby Daily Telegraph* ran a fascinating story headlined: "Elopement from Mickleover." However, the couple concerned was far from a Romeo and his Juliet. "The circumstances are by no means of a romantic character," warned the writer:

"The woman is the wife of a labourer in the employ of a well-known athlete, and the man with whom she had decamped being a waggoner, many years her junior. The husband has for some time suspected an undue intimacy between the pair, and on the night of the elopement was watching outside the house. He saw the youthful waggoner come down the street, minus his shoes, and enter his house, being let in by the woman. A short time afterwards both left the house together, and the deserted husband believes the runaways are now living in Derby."

It seemed that the husband was none too concerned and was "thinking of resorting to the practical method of a divorce to free himself entirely from the woman who has deserted him".

IN March 1884, Mickleover played host to the Coldstream Guards who held their annual steeplechase around the village. According to the *Derbyshire Times* there were 15 competitors "attired in the orthodox hunting scarlet and chimney-pot hat". The two-and-a-half-mile long course was marked out with white flags and, according to the paper: "The ground, owing to the recent rains, was very heavy, and a spirited gallop across a ploughed field sent the water flying high above the horses' heels. The finish was a broad brook, and the excitement of the contest might have afforded inspiration to such sporting pens as Whyte-Melville's or George Lawrence's."

JAMES Edwin Ellor, of Grandell, South Drive, Chain Lane, held a patent for more than 60 inventions. Among them were an exhaust system, a torpedo turbine, an internal combustion engine, propellers, cooling systems and many other engineering items.

IN its edition of 25 May 1934, the *Derby Telegraph* reported, with some excitement: "A nightingale has taken up residence in Bunker's Wood on the edge of Mickleover golf course. The wood lies between the main Uttoxeter and Burton roads, and the bird's song can be heard clearly from the footpath over the golf course from Keats Avenue to Mickleover." The report advised: "The best time to hear the songster is between 10.30pm and midnight."

It was believed to be the first nightingale to have visited the wood for several years. *Note:* In a map of 1882 this was spelled Buncars Wood.

IN 1933, the *Derby Evening Telegraph* told its readers that a house in Mickleover was named after a Chinese city. Mr and Mrs J. P. Rodell spent 19 years in China as missionaries with the Society of Friends and had named their home on Uttoxeter Road "Chengtu", after their last posting

IN early December 1931, *Derby Evening Telegraph* readers were learning about the "Mickleover Tramp Menace".

The Mickleover and District Ratepayers' Association had discussed the increasing problem at a meeting. Mr C. E. Williams said that he had "received complaints that numbers of tramps and unlicensed hawkers were making calls in the district and the unwelcome visitors were often abusive to women".

Williams asked that more police, preferably two more and in plain clothes, be assigned to the village and to neighbouring Littleover, which was similarly afflicted. Mr Williams told the newspaper: "Chain Lane and Western Road appeared to be the meeting place of people of the vagrant class." On his return home from the meeting he discovered that a caller had insulted his wife because she had refused his assistance.

IN August 1938, Harold Amery, of Station House, Mickleover, "killed an adder three feet six inches in length when it was about to enter his garden". Mr Amery had seen the snake from his house and was able to pierce its head with a garden fork "but not before it attempted to strike him". Mr Amery told the *Derby Evening Telegraph* that it he could not remember having previously seen an adder in Mickleover.

Station Road with its one pavement. In the distance can be seen the corner shop at the junction with Park Road.

Cutting the turf for the new St John the Evangelist church on Darwin Road in 1964.

The Duke of Edinburgh visits the new St John the Evangelist church.

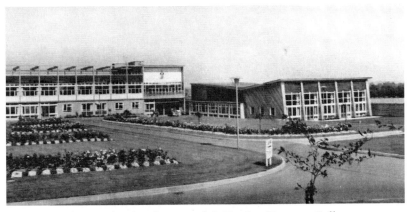

The completed Bishop Lonsdale Teacher Training College.

The ruins of the old windmill on Mill Lane, off Station Road.

1960s architecture on Inglewood Avenue.

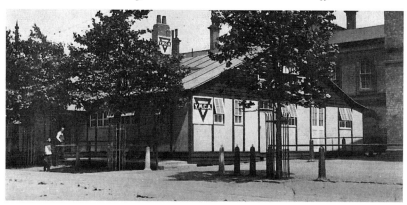

The Memorial Hut on Station Road, once used by the YMCA at Derby's LMS Station.

New House Farm on the western edge of the village.

20

A Growing Mickleover

The following businesses have supported publication of this book:

Devonshire Drive Post Office is owned by Joanne Jones, sub-postmistress for the past 18 years. Originally sited at 81 Devonshire Drive, in later years a subpostmaster, Jim Doncaster, moved it around the corner to 50 East Avenue, but still retained its name. He designed this post office so that there was a hairdresser attached, separated only by a partition wall, for his wife to have a hairdressing business, and that remains there today.

Past sub-postmasters have included Mr and Mrs Ted Chuds and Mr and Mrs Staton. Joanne Jones took over the post office in March

Inside Devonshire Drive Post Office. The counter area in 2004.

The counter area in 2012.

1996. From 1997 to 2004 (when the "Best Post Office" competition was ended) the business won awards for services to the community. Joanne has seen many changes within the Post Office network with many sadly closing. She says: "I am grateful for all the support I have received from the local community over the years. Long may it continue."

The Butler's Pantry is a quintessentially British tearoom and bistro in the heart of Mickleover. Overlooking the Old Square and steeped in history, it is hard to imagine this 300-year-old building was once a family home. Although it now has a more contemporary feel, the original beams can still be seen on the staircase.

The tearoom is a friendly and welcoming place to visit, and offers waiter service for breakfast, lunch and afternoon tea menus. There is a mix of traditional dishes alongside the more adventurous, as chef-proprietor Ralph Skripek is a renowned game chef and can be seen demonstrating game cookery at food fairs throughout the country.

In addition to the tearoom, the bistro offers private dining for parties between 12-22 guests and hosts regular speciality evenings including 'Wine Tasting & Dinner Evenings', 'Lobster & Seafood' and, of course, 'Taste of Game Nights'.

Ralph is also a local author who has published a game cookery book entitled *Wild Chef* that includes 21 seasonal game recipes and personal anecdotes of the great outdoors. Ralph has had the pleasure of cooking dinner for both Hilary Devey (ex-*Dragons' Den* and *Secret Millionaire*), at her palatial home in Staffordshire, and Clarissa Dickson Wright (from *Two Fat Ladies*) and has worked alongside many television celebrity chefs including Mike Robinson, Alan Coxon and

Tim Maddams from *River Cottage*. He has also been a guest chef on *BBC Radio Derby*, promoting local produce.

The Butler's Pantry is also recognised as one of the leading caterers in the Midlands and is extremely proud to be a nominated caterer for some of the most prestigious venues in the county, including National Trust properties. Catering services, bars and event planning from 12 to 500 guests can all be booked, everything from a traditional buffet, sit-down dinner, BBQ or afternoon tea service can be provided by their professional events team.

The Butler's Pantry is a proud winner of the *Theo Paphitis Small Business Sunday* award – being chosen by Theo himself – as a committed and thriving small business. This was a great honour and achievement.

For further details on the tearoom, bistro, outside catering services or cookery demonstrations telephone 01332 519007 or visit http://www.butlerspantryderby.co.uk/, or for their sister company http://www.thewildchef.co.uk/

Longcroft Boarding Kennels And Cattery, Staker Lane, Mickleover, Derby. I believe the cottage was built in 1911 by a local landowner for a Captain Piggin, to be used with surrounding land and stables as a stud farm (writes Rosemary Thomas). At that time Staker Lane had several pretty thatched cottages along the verges with just a single-track road. The now derelict buildings in the adjacent field to the east were used by a blacksmith to shoe the horses. The evidence for this I am continually digging up in my garden. I have several horseshoes, pieces of stirrups, lumps of iron and cinders. Someone who lived in the lane as a boy informed me that in the field behind the cottage Captain Piggin held a gymkhana for the whole village every year. He remembered that, during the war years, he threw objects at a picture of Hitler in order to win a prize, and both German and Italian POWs worked in the fields between the then stables and Watergo Lane. The property later passed to a Miss Martin who also kept horses and would ride out sidesaddle.

Romany gypsies visited the lane to collect willow branches from Watergo Lane to make clothes pegs. They painted peach stones that they sold as lucky charms. My informant told me that their caravans were immaculate, with goats and horses all well looked after and they were no trouble to anyone.

Longcroft passed to various people but has always been connected with horses, dogs and cats. The boarding kennels have been open for visiting guests for about 20 years and for the past 15 years with myself the current owner.

The kennels are now fully licenced by the local authority for 65 dogs and 30 cats. The staff are fully qualified in animal care including animal first-aid, providing a caring, professional service. We have pets of our own and understand how important they are as members of a family; we care for them as we would our own. Medication can be administered as required. Many elderly pets stay with us and we understand their special needs.

All kennels have heat lamps and the cattery is also heated. We have three enclosed exercise paddocks where the dogs run free, individually or family groups, at least three times daily. Animals receive lots of attention and play while with us. We also have several extra-large kennels for giant breeds or family groups. Our prices are very competitive and we use a grading by size system – available on request.

In order to keep change to a minimum it is our policy to feed the same food as the animals receive at home. A collection and delivery

service can be provided, subject to distance, and we have a fully equipped grooming room with an excellent groomer on the premises three days per week.

We have an open-door policy because we can guarantee we are always clean. Opening times are 9am – 12 noon and 2pm – 4.30pm Monday to Saturday, and 9am – 12 noon Sunday and Bank Holidays. Visitors will be made very welcome by the staff. The kennels provide a valuable service to the community and is open 365 days in the year. We can take pets at short notice for any length of stay – even day boys and girls! Why not visit our web site and view the gallery and reviews – www.longcroftboardingkennels.co.uk. Telephone 01332 518776 or e-mail rosemary-thomas@uwclub.net

Mickleover ChiroHealth Clinic was originally located in the Square in Mickleover but in 2004 moved to its current premises at 156 Station Road. In January 2008 the original owner emmigrated to New Zealand and the clinic was bought by its current owners Wayne and Tanuja Murray. Wayne is a chiropractor who has lived near Mickleover most of his life. He specialises in sports injuries and, as well as his practice at Mickleover ChiroHealth, has worked with both Derby County and Burton Albion football clubs. The 'team' at Mickleover ChiroHealth also include Carina Milne, also a chiropractor. Carina specialises in chiropractic for children and babies (as well as adults) and has been at the clinic since it started.

Other members of the team are Jayne Stokes and Judith Hyde. Jayne is a massage therapist who has been with the clinic for many years. Judith is our most recent addition and offers massage as well as holisitic and beauty therapy.

Although chiropractic is still a growing specialty in this country the people of Mickleover both young and old have embraced it, and the clinic is well known locally with an excellent reputation.

Revenge Hair Studio first opened its doors on 5 November 1998 and took pride of place at 13 The Square, Mickleover (writes Antony Davis). The fact that the building was number 13 and the phone number allocated to the business had "666" in it were pure coincidence and have caused many amusing comments over the years.

I originally called the salon *Storm* but when the company became limited in 2000 I was unable to copyright this name and decided to come up with an equally memorable replacement – *Revenge*, a name

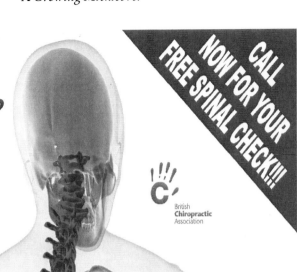

Do you suffer from any of the following?

- ✓ **Lower Back Pain**
- ✓ **Sciatica**
- ✓ **Neck Pain/Whiplash**
- ✓ **Joint Problems**
- ✓ **Sports Injuries**
- ✓ **Headaches**

Also Available:

Sports Massage Therapist

CALL NOW FOR YOUR FREE SPINAL CHECK!!!

British **Chiropractic** Association

If you are unsure about the benefits of chiropractic why not take advantage of our *free no obligation spinal check?*

Why Choose Us?
- Spacious Modern Clinic with *FREE* Parking
- Same Day Late & Emergency Appointments
- Assessment & Treatment in 1st Session
- From Babies to Adults We Can Help!

MickleoverChirohealthClinic.com

Wayne Murray B.Sc (Hons) M.Sc, D.C | Carina Milne B.Sc (Hons), D.C

Call on 01332 511119 or visit us at
156 Station Road, Mickleover, DE3 9FL

Member of the
General Chiropractic
Council

that people would not forget – and I secured all rights to use this brand for hairdressing.

The concept of my salon was based on an idea to recreate a city-centre environment based within a thriving village location. There are only two staff at Revenge – myself and my salon partner, Amanda Bull – and we have worked seamlessly together to create the thriving salon we have today. We are both local people, grew up in Mickleover and went to school here. We also have a vast amount of joint experience and have trained and worked in well-known city-centre salons, with the emphasis being made on creative cutting and colouring techniques.

Our wonderful, loyal client base consists of trendy teenagers right through to stylish older people and we hope to serve them for many years to come.

Foxy Lady Beauty Salon at 1a The Square, Mickleover, has been owned and run by mother and daughter 'team' Carolyn Keightley and Claire Cummings for the past 16 years.

Carolyn says: "In 1998 we bought what was then a very small business and have, over the years, developed it into what it is today – one of Derbyshire's leading beauty salons. We are *Guinot* accredited and carry out the world-renowned *Guinot* facial treatments. We offer an extensive list of treatments that are updated and added to regularly.

Our therapists are fully qualified and between us all we offer a very professional service in a comfortable, friendly and relaxed environment."

Mickleover-born-and-bred Phil Bowler established **Phil Bowler Garage Services Ltd** on Uttoxeter Road, in 1996. Phil spent the next four years building up a highly reputable business, offering the local community and surrounding areas assistance in vehicle repairs, MOTs, tyres, exhausts and servicing.

As the business grew, in 2000 Phil moved it to larger premises on Station Road, Mickleover, where he was able to set up his own MOT station. Phil and his team of highly qualified trained mechanics continue Phil's philosophy to offer an outstanding service to new and old customers alike, while endeavouring to offer the best prices around for all types of servicing and tyre replacement. Testament to this is the high volume of loyalty shown by customers who Phil has looked after for more than 17 years.

THE origins of **Hackwood Farm** go back more than 200 years and we are dedicated to protecting and nurturing its family-run working farm heritage. This is demonstrated by our ever-growing variety of livestock including sheep, chickens, ducks and our much-loved Pietrain x Gloucester Old Spot pigs.

In addition, our farm also has the benefit of ten stables with livery and a traditional orchard containing a well established range of old variety apple, pear and damson trees which are harvested to produce homemade jams, chutneys, pies and crumbles.

Our passion to offer local produce of the highest quality also helps to celebrate everything that is wonderful about rural Derbyshire – from its mouthwatering food to its beautiful countryside and unique history.

Did you know that we now have a small children's farm at Hackwood!

It's important to us that children have an opportunity to see, hear and smell farm animals and understand where their food comes from. Animal feed is available to buy.

Daily we serve freshly prepared specials including breakfast snacks, light lunches and afternoon teas using locally sourced ingredients from the farm shop and other trusted regional suppliers. We have a selection of cakes on offer including a wide variety of gluten free. Takeaway tea, coffee and cakes are available if you're in a rush or on the move.

Choose from a wide range of cheeses, displayed as traditional rounds, cured meats, pasties, pies and pâtés, olives, sun-dried tomatoes and salami, quiche, sausage rolls and much more.

If you fancy leaving the cooking to us, we have a great selection of homemade ready meals, either for one or to host a whole dinner party.

Our butcher, Rob, has been working hard to create a wonderful range of meats using only the very best from local farmers. The quality of meat at Hackwood Farm is second to none, based on the principal of high welfare and local suppliers. We offer an alternative to buying bright red meat in plastic trays – our steaks are 28-day matured and full of flavour. Buying meat from us means that not only are you supporting farmers within a few miles of home, but you can also ensure that these animals haven't travelled long distances and aren't stressed. Not only is that satisfying from a welfare point of view but the flavour and quality is vastly improved.

Our blackboards will tell you which farmers have supplied us that week and you can place orders for that special occasion too. And we offer a Veg Box delivery service, or you can collect from the farm. Just let us know your favourite seasonal veg and we'll have a box ready for you. For further information contact: georgina.bennett@ hackwoodfarm.com. Also, Hackwood Hampers, packed full of local Derbyshire produce – perfect for presents! Our hampers contain a large percentage of items that can be sourced only in Derbyshire, therefore making them a thoughtful and unique gift for friends and family UK wide. Build your own Hamper – Please ask staff for details.

For enquiries and bookings please contact Georgina, info@ hackwoodfarm.com.

Mickleover Railway Station.

Freckleton's Post Office, Uttoxeter Road.

The Mickleover Court Hotel on Etwall Road.

GNT's premises on Etwall Road. The company is a global market leader in colouring food.

This charming cottage stood opposite the Mickleover Court Hotel.

Now home to a car wash, Pick-Kwik was long a feature at the top of Station Road.

Mickleover Old Hall, Orchard Street.

Overfields Lodge, The Green.

Mickleover's new library on Holly End Road.